The Green Red Green

THE GREEN
RED GREEN

(MADE ALMOST ENTIRELY FROM RECYCLED MATERIAL)

Doubleday Canada

Doubleday Canada and colophon are registered trademarks of Random House of Canada Limited

Library and Archives Canada Cataloguing in Publication

Smith, Steve, 1945-
    The green Red Green : made almost entirely from recycled material / Red Green.

Issued also in electronic format.
ISBN 978-0-385-67858-2

    I. Title.

PS8587.M589A6 2012   C818'.5402   C2012-902429-5

Cover and text design: Leah Springate
Cover image: Roy Timm
Printed and bound in the USA

Published in Canada by Doubleday Canada,
a division of Random House of Canada Limited

Visit Random House of Canada Limited's website:
www.randomhouse.ca

10 9 8 7 6 5 4 3 2 1

DEDICATION

I'd like to dedicate this book to a lot of people, first and foremost, the Lodge members—the ones who stepped up early in support of the whole Red Green project and then sustained that support through the ridicule of friends and family. These people are special, and often in a good way. These are fearless people. They aren't the kind to wait to see what others are going to do, in life or the buffet line. When they see something they sort of like, or at least are curious about, they get involved. It's much easier to jump on a bandwagon once it's rolling than to climb up there while it's parked over a septic bed in the hopes of some movement. So I give special thanks to the members of Possum Lodge who, like the first people to take their bathing suits off in the hot tub, add a feeling of excitement, risk and urgency to life.

Next I would like to thank the people who bought the original versions of each of the three books that went into this one. Without them this book would not have happened. It's an attempt to build on success. Nobody builds on failure other than politicians and Zsa Zsa Gabor. So thanks to all of you out there who bought this crap when it was fresh.

But the largest portion of my gratitude goes to all of the people out there who did not buy any of these books. According to the sales reports, there are millions of you. That's what created the impetus for this book. The potential of being able to reach new customers with not only this book, but also the subtle message that if they refuse to buy it, it will not go away but will just keep coming back in different forms until they eventually surrender. We could have called it *Dracula's Tome*. But we didn't. So to all of you potential customers out there, please buy this book now and end the horror.

FOREWORD
(Count 'em)

Quando Omni Flunkus Moritati

FORWARD

Signified by the letter *D*; found between Reverse, Neutral, and Low; and a better life choice than any of the alternatives, with the exception of Park.

INTRODUCTION

We wanted to come out with a new book but were unable to find a formula that accommodated the time frame set by the publisher, given the fundamental inertness of the author. So instead, we are coming out with this old book in a new form. Every man knows it's easier to support your wife's cosmetic surgery than it is to find someone more attractive.

In truth, this is actually a combination of three of our old books with the odd new word or punctuation mark thrown in, just to keep you on your toes, and also to qualify us for government subsidies. You'll be pleased to know that we've done a lot of editing to get rid of the bad, boring stuff, so as you're reading it, I hope you'll appreciate that it's way better than it could have been.

Of course, whenever you remove inadequacies, you run the risk of making the good stuff look worse without the crap there to lower the average. But that's all just part of the precarious nature of being in the publishing business—which doesn't concern me, as I was given a healthy advance.

In any case, our intent was to go back to the abandoned mines of our old books and see if we could find enough nuggets to fill a new book which would allow our actions and attitudes to compromise yet another generation. I think we've succeeded, but only time will tell.

We hope you enjoy this book, but then again, we're also hoping for world peace.

Red Green

CONTENTS OF TABLE

The following were all in the drawers of the table I sat at when I wrote this book.

THE IMPORTANCE OF BEING HANDY

I have this theory that the human brain is a muscle rather than an organ. And as a muscle, it gets stronger with use and, conversely, atrophies through idleness. People who don't do any thinking in their lives as a way of keeping their brain fresh for old age are seriously misinformed. You're much better off using your brain as often as possible. Even once or twice a day if you can manage it.

And of course, choosing what to use your brain on is very important. You don't want to waste your time on things that are irrelevant or boring or beyond your comprehension. For most of us, abstract mathematics or nuclear physics is a complete waste of time. I recommend that you become a handyman. The mental agility required first to diagnose why the refrigerator isn't working and then to acquire the correct part, remove the old one without breaking everything around it, and install the new one is fantastic exercise. And that's not to mention what pinching your thumb in the door hinge does for your language skills. Then there's the whole creative challenge of explaining to your wife that the refrigerator couldn't be fixed so you threw it out but thank goodness you didn't waste money by bringing in a professional repairman.

These are the kinds of skills that will keep your mind agile well into old age. Plus you'll have a lot more free time because your wife will refrain from telling you when something needs fixing.

WHY DUCT TAPE

I want to try to help all you ladies understand the things we men do. For example, the way we fix things with duct tape. Like, say, the mirror that fell off the car.

Now, I know a lot of you would take the car into a garage and have it fixed properly and looking good an hour and sixty bucks later. Whereas your handyman does it in ten minutes with about seven cents' worth of duct tape and it is some kind of ugly. But let's go behind the actions and try to examine the reasoning.

First of all, what is the value of the vehicle? Are we talking about a 1981 Cordoba with four hundred thousand miles and a real bad cough? Does it make sense to spend sixty bucks on a car that you can replace for fifty? And why take an hour to fix it if it can be done in ten minutes? After putting four hundred thousand miles on this unit, you really don't owe it any more of your time. And why repair the mirror back to original quality? It just makes the rest of the vehicle look bad.

There's no sense in having the repair job last longer than the equipment. So instead of criticizing your man for slapping the mirror back on with duct tape, why don't you compliment him on his brain power? After all, he now has fifty minutes to kill and an extra sixty bucks in his pocket.

SMELL OF SUCCESS

As we men get older, it gets more and more difficult to attract women. We lose our physique and our hair. We wear glasses and hearing aids. And we forget what we were saying in mid-sentence. It eventually gets so bad, our only hope of attracting a member of the opposite sex is to make sure we smell good and then sit near a woman with a big nose.

HOW TO GET AND KEEP THAT ALL-IMPORTANT FIRST JOB

Assert yourself. Show confidence. Nobody wants to hire a wuss. Arrive late for the interview and try to look a little rough. Don't give the false impression that you'll be getting up early to groom yourself before coming to work. Once you're in the boss's office, show you're interested in the job by asking important questions. How much does it pay? When can you take holidays? Does anybody check on you when you phone in sick? Are there any better jobs available at other companies? How often can you get a raise? How much severance will you get when you're fired? How many relatives and friends are covered by the medical plan? Which office supplies is it okay to steal? What's in it for me?

If by some chance you are not hired for the job, start legal action. So far, incompetents are still a minority in this country and are therefore protected by the Canadian Human Rights Act. Another thing you have going for you is that you have no idea how to do the job and thereby qualify for a government-assisted training plan. If you are competent, knowledgeable, and experienced, you're out of luck.

Once you've got the job, try to fit in and get along with your new co-workers. Remember, everybody enjoys it when you make a joke about the size of their belly. Always bear in mind that you're the new person, so don't tell everybody how to do their jobs until the second day. But don't be too laid back either. Get your co-workers' respect by forming a union. If they already have a union, form another one—one with a militia. Sit at the end of

3

the table in the cafeteria, open your lunch box, and pull out a really expensive sandwich, like roast beef or shrimp or anything on a kaiser. Be sociable. Ask your co-workers what they are eating. Ask to try some.

Show an interest in your co-workers. Question them about what they do, what it pays, and how a person would go about getting their job—theoretically, of course.

Be a team player: get on the winning team and let them carry you.

The hardest trick is to believe in yourself. You're no better and no worse than the people you're working with, and there's no reason for them to treat you any differently than they treat each other. Keep that in mind in everything you say and do and they'll never know this is your first job. Even though you're in your mid-forties.

THE GREAT BLOOD SHORTAGE

It seems to me that there's an inherent design flaw in the structure of the human body. If you imagine that every muscle and organ is a tiny engine and the fuel is blood, then you can see that there is really not enough fuel to have all the engines running at the same time. That's why it's so difficult to watch television and think simultaneously. But with a book, you can stop reading and put it down for a minute and think about exactly why Jack and Jill went up that hill.

Because of this insufficient blood supply, the human brain must prioritize the muscles and organs to decide which ones should get the blood at any particular moment, why they need it, and what they plan to do with it once they have it. If you had special glasses that detected hemoglobin or whatever, you would be able to look at a man and see where the blood is going and have a pretty good idea of his intentions. You'd also be able to see why it's difficult for him to think about anything else. He doesn't have enough fuel for that. If he had more blood, he'd be able to see all the options and make an informed choice. Mind you, that might make him less of a man.

PARTY POLITICS

All right, you were at a party last night with your wife or your girlfriend or your female companion. And today you're being informed that you didn't have as good a time as you recall. This is because your partner did not appreciate you ignoring her totally, or flirting with other women, or doing that party trick where you play "God Save the Queen" by making loud, wet noises with parts of your body. It's surprising how some people fail to enjoy live entertainment, but the point is that you're now in trouble and you need some way to patch up the situation.

Whenever you can, blame the booze. Just tell her that you were over-served and weren't acting like yourself. If you don't drink, that's unfortunate because it forces you to lie. You'll have to blame your behaviour on being really upset about, say, the death of a close friend. But just remember that when she asks you who died, you're going to be expected to come up with a name. Saying "old what's his name" won't cut it. What I do is name a friend I don't mind never seeing again.

Or you could take the strong route and just tell her that's the way you are at parties and that'll be the end of that. And the end of going to another party with her. Or anywhere with her. Or anywhere with anybody.

DO IT BECAUSE YOU DON'T NEED TO

Life is like a car—there's only one driver's seat. And you want to be in that driver's seat as often as possible. Most of us get a shot at the driver's seat when we get older, after we've retired and have done all our major spending and set up enough of a pension to support ourselves. That's the ideal time to get a job.

It can be any job, but it's better if you deal with the public, like say in a store or a post office or something. Because the beauty of this job is that you don't need it. You can conduct yourself in any way you feel is appropriate. Be rude to people. Ignore them. See how mad you can make them. Use this job as your way of getting back at all the stupid clerks and officials you've had to put up with your whole life. You'll get rid of all your frustrations (actually, you're just passing them on). You'll get up anxious to go to work, and you'll come home refreshed and energized. Being cantankerous will extend your life.

Sure, you'll eventually be fired, but they'll have to pay you severance, and then you can go get a job you need even less.

HOW TO BE A GOOD PASSENGER (BECAUSE YOUR LIFE MATTERS)

If you're a passenger in a moving car, with any luck somebody is driving. Drivers have a lot of responsibility. They shouldn't be penalized for volunteering to stay sober at the party. They shouldn't have to listen to you pointing out oncoming vehicles or red lights, or overdoing it on the random screams. Don't bug the driver. He already has his hands full—of beer nuts. So here are a few tips that can save your life, especially if you don't have an accident.

Sit Comfortably

When you're hunched forward, frantically scanning the approaching horizon with your fingernails dug deep into the armrest, it implies that you are not totally convinced of the driver's competence. But you have to trust him. If he says he knows his way home in the dark and doesn't need headlights, then you have to trust his judgment. Lean back, undo your belt, and pretend you're asleep.

Watch Your Topics

It's often a good idea to talk to the driver. It keeps him awake and stops him from singing. Just be careful what you talk about or it could be taken as an insult. In general, don't talk about traffic accidents. Don't mention your uncle, who also drives with one finger and a beer gut draped over the wheel, and how he hit a pothole and jammed the turn signal arm deeply into his navel. Don't mention the fog or the ice. If the driver hasn't noticed them, you're better off starting a prayer and trying to relax your shoulders while you brace for impact. If you have to talk, talk to other passengers or to yourself, perhaps about the weather or if anyone has taken courses in first aid or trauma treatment.

Don't Touch Stuff

Cars are designed so that one person can operate all the controls. Just because you can reach buttons on the dashboard, that does not mean they are legally your vehicular responsibility. The radio tuner and volume controls are Driver Only. As is the heater. The comfort of the driver is paramount. If he's warm enough, you just have to sit there quietly with your tongue frozen to the window winder. Don't touch the sunroof controls, the high beam switch, or the gearshift. If you have to adjust things or you go crazy, wear clothes with lots of buttons and zippers. Worry beads might help. You could also adjust the passenger seat a few times, but remember, a little of that goes a long way.

Don't Keep Looking at the Map

What kind of a message does that send? You think the goof is lost. And you could get motion sickness. Remember, vomiting never adds to the enjoyment of a trip.

Don't Be Embarrassed

As a passenger, you can sometimes get embarrassed by certain habits your driver practices: splashing pedestrians, or not signalling turns, or cutting across four lanes of traffic to run over an apple, or side-swiping hitchhikers. Once embarrassed, a passenger is prone to say things to the driver that will lead to a difference of opinion and a ninety-mile-an-hour hair-pulling incident. And any traffic expert will tell you that's asking for trouble. Instead, wear a disguise like a false nose and glasses, or if yours are already false, wear a real nose and glasses. That way, other drivers will not be able to recognize you at the trial.

Avoid eye contact with other motorists, no matter how hard they're honking or staring at you through the windshield, screaming, "Stop! Please stop and let me off!" If you do accidentally lock eyes, shrug your shoulders to imply helplessness or hold up your arms so it looks like you're handcuffed, and they will assume you're being kidnapped and focus their anger and lawsuits on the driver.

Another good trick to deter angry people is to dress like a cop. Or even better, become a cop.

Ride Defensively

As you sit quietly, watching the miles and bicyclists fly past your window, plan your escape route. Then you're ready in the event of an accident—or a really big guy in an overturned tractor-trailer coming over to rearrange your driver's face.

When you see an impending collision because the driver is passing on a hill or bouncing off guardrails or jumping a lift bridge, pretend you dropped something on the floor and when you go down to get it, stay there until the vehicle comes to a complete stop. It doesn't usually take long. Then say, "Thanks, this is close enough. I'll walk from here."

If the vehicle is on fire, it's okay to just say, "Thanks, see ya."

Don't Point Stuff Out

If you're older than eight (and if you're reading this book, that's unlikely), you should not be yelling "Cow!" every time you pass a cow. The world is an interesting place, but a running commentary from you doesn't make it more interesting and may distract your driver from oncoming traffic, oncoming guardrails, or oncoming canals. So avoid the temptation to keep up a running commentary like this: "Oh look, that barn is burnt. That was some fire. Hey, look at that apple stand you drove through. Hey, look at that cop waving at you . . . Look at that cop shooting at you! Look, a cow. That's some cow. She doesn't look happy, does she? Maybe if you hit the windshield wipers, you'll dislodge her . . ."

Twelve More Things You Should Not Do

1) Eat an unsliced watermelon.
2) Do your rosary.
3) Grab the steering wheel.

4) Stand up.

5) Slam your foot down on an imaginary brake pedal and whimper.

6) Start a singalong. Especially of "Ninety-nine Bottles of Beer on the Wall."

7) Pour coffee for the driver while holding the cup over his lap.

8) Unwrap a kielbasa that's older than the vehicle.

9) Pick your nose. Or anyone's nose.

10) Read over your will.

11) Offer to drive.

12) Not offer to drive.

LIFE IS SPORT

Now, I know that a lot of women like sports, but the vast majority of sports fans are men. And predominantly middle-aged men. We're the ones sprawled out on the family room couch with an ottoman handy to catch the overflow. We're the ones who will watch any sport, anytime, anywhere. And I think I know why: in sports, you are always living "in the moment." While what happened in the past might have some relevance and what will happen in the future is tinged with hope, sports are mainly focused on what is happening RIGHT NOW. Middle-aged men love that. That's where we want to be: living in the moment. Not living in the past, where we had more of everything, from freedom to hairstyle choices, and could be criticized for our uninspired career choices after graduation or our inappropriate behaviour at last night's party. Not living in the future, where we will look back at our current physical deterioration as the good old days. No, we don't want to think about that. The truth is, we don't want to think about anything. But hey, that's what sports on television are for.

FORGOT? NOW WHAT?

Your anniversary, which you seem to recall is coming up, is not coming up. It's gone by. It was yesterday.

Now, you could just admit that you forgot about the anniversary and you feel real bad about it and it doesn't mean you don't care and would she please forgive you? But she won't. So instead, tell her that you had to postpone the anniversary because the special gift you got for her couldn't be delivered until the weekend. Which gives you until the weekend to buy something. If you then forget to buy her the present . . . well, you're on your own.

Or pull out your wallet and find last year's calendar on one of those little cards and point to it and say, "There's your problem: I had the right day, just the wrong year. I guess next year we'll have to celebrate our anniversary twice." That might work. If it doesn't, you may not be celebrating even once.

SILENCE, PLEASE

In my early twenties I was in a rock band. We played different kinds of music, but all of it really loud. The slogan "How do we do it? Volume!" was a pretty good description of our approach. When you're loud, you don't get criticized. Or at least you don't hear the criticism. But that was some time ago. Now I don't like anything loud. I need to be able to hear what my wife is saying. I've learned that it's better for everyone if I hear her the first time. Before I buy something else that we don't need. And before she commits me to a social function. Or an institution.

I used to like loud things, like rock music and dragsters and explosions. Now I like quiet things—like babies not crying and phones not ringing and salesmen not knocking. If I worked at the airport wearing those silencer earmuffs, I'd probably leave them on all the time. Except, of course, when my wife is talking.

HOW TO BUILD A SELF-CLEANING CAR

Here's an easy way to build an automatic, self-contained mobile washer that keeps your car continuously clean. Just like going to the car wash—except it's free and you don't have to go the car wash.

You will need a whole bunch of sprinklers. It's that simple. You'll find them on people's front lawns long after they've gone to bed. Mount the sprinklers all over the car using bolts and rivets, or if you work for the government, you may have the time to sit and magnetize them. But if you like the chrome look, use duct tape.

Attach all the sprinklers together using garden hoses from the source mentioned above. Now you need a supply of water— one that moves with the car, so you can wash your vehicle on the move. And you have a source right inside the engine compartment: namely, the water pump and the radiator. All you have to do is tap into them.

Don't forget that a mobile car wash does not have an unlimited supply of water, so what you're going to have to do is recycle it (and I don't mean the way people adrift at sea recycle their water). Measure the exact outside circumference of your car and get exactly that much eavestroughing. Attach the eavestroughs all the way around the car to catch any runoff. Run a hose from the intake side of the water pump into the eavestroughs to put the wash water back into the radiator, creating a completely closed system—except, of course, for evaporation. You can compensate for that by leaving your car out in the rain.

WHAT TOOLS DO PROS HAVE IN THEIR TOOL KITS? AND WHAT DO I HAVE IN MINE?

The home handyman usually has between forty and sixty different tools in his tool box. A professional builder or carpenter carries as many as three hundred different tools in his tool kit. I carry five.

The Red Green Very Portable Tool Kit

1) Hammer
2) Saw
3) Screwdriver
4) Pliers
5) Roll of duct tape

Those five tools have everything I need to fix a loose chair, rewire a socket, or add an addition to the house. Here's a list of all the tools you can buy if you're absolutely made of money. Beside each is the tool I use to do the same job.

Well-Stocked Tool Box	My Tool Box
Hammer — — — — — — — — — —	Hammer
Saw — — — — — — — — — — —	Saw
3 screwdrivers (slot head) — — — —	Screwdriver
3 Phillips head screwdrivers — — —	Hammer
3 Robertson head screwdrivers — —	Hammer
3 chisels — — — — — — — — — —	Screwdriver
Crowbar — — — — — — — — — —	Hammer
Wrench — — — — — — — — — —	Hammer
Hacksaw — — — — — — — — — —	Saw or hammer
Mitre saw — — — — — — — — —	Saw
Sabre saw — — — — — — — — —	Saw
Reciprocating saw — — — — — — —	Saw or hammer
Hole saw — — — — — — — — — —	Hammer
Metal ruler — — — — — — — — —	Metal edge of Saw blade
2 slip-joint pliers — — — — — — —	Pliers
Lineman's pliers — — — — — — —	Pliers
Channel-type pliers, Vise-Grip pliers, end-cutting nippers, needle-nose pliers, long-nose pliers, pipe wrench, adjustable wrench, ratchet wrench, open-end, box-end wrench set, Allen wrench set — — —	Pliers
Rubber mallet — — — — — — — —	Hammer
Wood mallet — — — — — — — — —	Hammer
Nail set and nail punch — — — — —	Hammer
Electric drill — — — — — — — — —	Hammer
Plane — — — — — — — — — — —	Screwdriver
Putty knife — — — — — — — — —	Screwdriver
Scraper — — — — — — — — — —	Screwdriver
Soldering iron — — — — — — — —	Duct tape
Propane torch, solder — — — — —	Duct tape
Wood glue — — — — — — — — —	Duct tape

Hot glue gun — — — — — — —	Duct tape
Staple gun — — — — — — — —	Duct tape
Compass — — — — — — — — —	Duct tape roll
Router and router bits — — — — —	Screwdriver
Carpenter's level — — — — — — —	Eyeball
T-square — — — — — — — — —	Eyeball
Tape measure — — — — — — — —	Eyeball
Pipe cutter — — — — — — — —	Saw
Metal snips — — — — — — — —	Saw
C-clamp — — — — — — — — —	Nephew
Vise — — — — — — — — — —	Nephew
Wire cutters — — — — — — — —	Pliers
Wire-stripping tool — — — — — —	Pliers
Fuse puller — — — — — — — —	Pliers
Electrician's pliers — — — — — —	Pliers
Connecting nuts — — — — — —	Duct tape
Fuses — — — — — — — — — —	Pocketful of change
Circuit tester — — — — — — — —	Nephew's finger
Lathe — — — — — — — — — —	I don't build round things
Power jointer — — — — — — —	I don't joint things
Power drill press — — — — — —	Hammer
Grinder — — — — — — — — —	Hammer
Belt sander — — — — — — — —	Hammer
Pad sander — — — — — — — —	Hammer
Various files (wood and metal) — —	Screwdriver
Toilet plunger — — — — — — —	Nephew

I think you can see that my tool list proves a point I have always lived by: imagination costs nothing.

B&B BLUES

We're friends with a retired couple who have turned their house into a bed and breakfast. So unsurprisingly, my wife and I end up discussing the possibility of doing the same thing. That's a natural reaction. Whenever someone you know does something that you haven't done, you start considering it. That's why whenever you're selling some product that's completely worthless, the first sale is so important. Now, I don't know if my wife is going to push this bed and breakfast thing, but if so, I plan to fight it all the way. I don't like strangers in my house at any time, and letting them stay overnight is really asking for trouble. I'm going to hear strange noises and snippets of conversations and imagine what's going on in there. And who came up with the concept of giving them breakfast? That's not the high point of my day, either physically or emotionally. I'll be awake all night listening to potential tribal rituals, and then I'm expected to greet these transients at the bottom of the stairs with a smile and an omelette. It's more than a coincidence that the emergence of bed and breakfasts is concurrent with the increase in domestic violence.

DUMPSTER COTTAGE

Everybody likes to have someplace they can go to get away from it all, or get away from the law or whatever. But not everyone can afford a cottage, so here's a handyman project that will fit almost any budget. I'm assuming you have a piece of land somewhere, but even if you don't, it's a big country and they're not going to check every square mile every year, so you'll get at least one season out of wherever you build.

Step One

Call the biggest garbage collection agency in your region and ask them to drop off the biggest dumpster bin they have. It must have a heavy lid. Tell them you'll be clearing a property and will have a lot of garbage for them to come and get when it's done. In most cases, they will deliver the dumpster and leave it for no charge. Make sure they set it down between two big trees with high crotches. (High crotches are very important for almost everything you do outdoors.)

See Diagram A:

Step Two

You will need two spare tires off a car or a small truck. (If you don't have any sitting out on your porch, you can swipe them from the trunks of BMWs, because people who drive those cars would never change their own tires anyway.) Next, you must remove the tires from the rims. Gas stations have special equipment just for that, but you could try it with a crowbar and an oar. The easiest way is just to burn them off. Leave the area while they're burning. You should have no trouble finding your way back—just follow your nose. Scrape the residue off the wheel rims and attach them to opposite sides of the dumpster as shown in Diagram B.

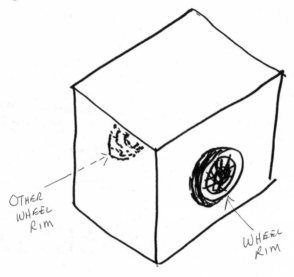

OTHER WHEEL RIM

WHEEL RIM

I recommend that you weld them on or drill holes and bolt them. Or you may want to use the Handyman's Secret Weapon—duct tape. These rims have to support the entire weight of a dumpster, so use lots of tape.

Step Three

Cut a door and a window in each side of the dumpster that has a rim. I recommend using an acetylene torch, but you can use a tempered axe or even a chainsaw if you really like sparks. Once that's done, move your living room furniture into the dumpster, set it on the floor, and bolt it into place. Lamps can be glued to tables. Next, wind your jumper cables around your appliances and hook them up to your car battery to magnetize them. Then bring them into the dumpster as well and stick them on the wall as shown in Diagram C. Attach your bedroom furniture to the inside of the lid of the dumpster with self-tapping screws. The fourth wall can be done as a family room or den or whatever suits your particular lifestyle. Again, all furnishings must be fastened securely to the wall.

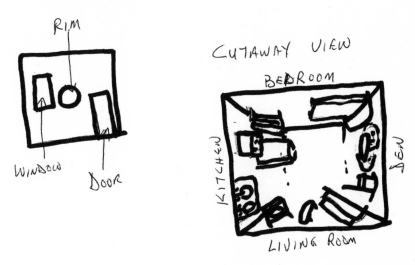

Step Four

To lift the dumpster up into the tree, you'll need a long chain or thick rope attached to the top. We tried it with a garden hose and I wouldn't recommend it. Rubber can really sting.

Take the rope and swing it over something high and strong, like an overhanging tree branch or railway bridge. Attach the other end to your van as in Diagram D. As you drive away, the rope will lift the dumpster up in the air. Unless the dumpster is heavier, in which case it will lift the van in the air. To avoid this problem, invite your overweight relatives over and stuff them into the van first. Drive forward slowly until the dumpster is in the air with the rims over the crotches of the tree. Back up until the rims drop into place, securing the dumpster.

Step Five

Get in and enjoy your summer. Sit in the living room and amuse yourself with your favourite television shows. When you need something from the kitchen, just walk toward it and the dumpster will rotate, bringing the kitchen to you. Same thing when it's bedtime or you need some quiet time in the den. Just walk toward whichever room you want. It's that simple.*

---

* Not recommended for Dutch elm trees or hillsides.

PROTESTING TOO MUCH

I was doing something on my computer the other day when suddenly a notice popped up in the middle of the screen saying, "You have performed an illegal operation! This program will be shut down!" What is that? An illegal operation? I pressed a button on my computer. Is that against the law now? This seems way over the top to me. I think it's a device created by the people who make these computers to cover their own mistakes. Obviously there's a glitch in the software that triggers a problem, and instead of creating a sign that says, "We screwed up by selling you this computer before we got the bugs out of it," they went with "You have performed an illegal operation!"

It's not a bad move, actually. Maybe you should try that in your own life. When your wife criticizes you, you just say, "You have performed an illegal operation! This conversation will be shut down!" And then go out. But first, make sure you have a house key in your pocket.

HOW TO BUY A HOME

Thinking of buying a new home? Or an old home? Or a cottage? Here are some things to watch out for when buying something that is going to put you in hock for the rest of your days.

Good Signs

- The owners are still in the country and alive.
- No large animal droppings are in the attic.
- There's glass in all the windows.

- It was not built on an ancient tribal burial ground, disturbing many graves.
- You're allowed to inspect all the rooms.
- Nothing breaks off when you touch it.
- It's more than fifty feet from all major airports, railways, dumpsites, and active volcanoes.

Bad Signs

- The word "REDRUM!" is carved in the walls.
- Their grandfather is included in the price.
- The real estate agent warns you not to walk in the middle of the floors, where it's soft.
- The sellers are "very motivated" to sell because they fear for their children's safety.
- There are high-water marks on the basement walls.
- The kitchen appliances are turquoise.
- There are bullet holes in the bathroom.
- The real estate agent says you can't flush the toilet until after you've bought the place.
- The house has been treated for termites nine times in the past two years.

NORTH OF FORTY

I want to talk to you guys who are celebrating your fiftieth birthday, or are just recovering from the hangover. You'll know what I'm talking about when they bring you your birthday cake and tell you that each candle represents a decade.

When we reach mid-life, most of us review our accomplishments and take stock of our careers, our family situation, and our position in the community, and often we conclude that life stinks and we really blew it. But I say we should look on the bright side: everybody's life stinks. Nobody gets what they want. Millionaires wish they were billionaires. Married guys wish they were playboys, and playboys wish they could find someone worth marrying. Maybe you regret not marrying your first sweetheart. Well, don't forget that you're not sweet sixteen anymore, and neither is she. If you passed each other on the street today, you'd both think, "Boy, some people really let themselves go."

So if you're feeling your life is over and you blew it, remember— it's only half over, and you only half blew it. And then get out there and finish the job.

HOW NOT TO DRIVE LIKE YOUR DAD

No one in your family has the nerve to tell you, so I will. I've seen you driving around town, turning without signalling or driving too slowly, turning right from the left-turn lane, parking your car half on the sidewalk. The fact is, you're starting to drive like your dad. Nothing is scarier than a little man in a big car, peeking over the dashboard with a sour look on his face.

Now, some say losing your driving skills is just nature's way of thinning the herd, but I say give it up. And I say that knowing you won't. Because every man I'm referring to figures I'm referring to someone else.

At your age, you really only drive to your job, your lodge, your grocery store, the gas station, and maybe your church. Plot out each route carefully and memorize all the proper procedures to get there using turn signals and brakes. Try to stay up near the speed limit. It's printed on big signs at the side of the road. Once you have that circuit down, you won't be such a menace anymore.

HOW TO BE THE LIFE AND SOUL OF THE PARTY

Treasure Hunt

When you're at someone's house and she's busy in the kitchen with some type of fire, pry off one of the furnace vents and drop in a really old egg. Replace the vent and wait for the fun to start. The game is over when somebody finds the egg or the guests pass out or the hostess insists it's time for Grandpa to see a specialist.

Doggy, Doggy, Who's Got the Bone?

For this game, everyone sits in a circle or an ellipse, depending on the room's shape. One contestant leaves the room, and while he's gone, one of the people in the circle consumes seven or eight martinis in as many minutes. The contestant returns to the room and tries to guess who had the drinks. He is allowed to check your breath for traces of olives, ask you to perform a motor skill, or demand that you sing one of the up-tempo numbers from *Mary Poppins*. Although the first round is pretty obvious, the game gets more difficult as the evening progresses. The game is over when you run out of martinis or the paramedics arrive.**

Chainsaw Puzzle

Exactly like a jigsaw puzzle. Well, not *exactly*. Instead of a jigsaw, you use a chainsaw to make the puzzle. And instead of a picture of some Mediterranean village, you saw up an old chair, a broken

---

** Publisher's note: Do not under any circumstances ever play this game.

freezer, or a used car. And you don't bother putting it back together again—that's boring. But like a jigsaw puzzle, a chainsaw puzzle is frequently missing one piece at the end . . . although it's usually a piece of someone who stood too close.

Ego Pursuit

Get out one of the popular trivia games and divide the players into teams. Play the game as per the instructions, with the teams taking turns asking each other questions. The game is played exactly as explained by the manufacturer with one important difference—ALL ANSWERS WILL BE ACCEPTED AS CORRECT.

Example

> *Team 1:* Who was the twenty-third president of the United States?
> *Team 2:* Colonel Sanders.
> *Team 1:* Correct.

or

> *Team 2:* What is the name of the fifth planet from the sun?
> *Team 1:* Stan.
> *Team 2:* Right on!

Each team is also obliged to compliment the answer.

Example

> *Team 1:* What is the main ingredient in Hollandaise sauce?
> *Team 2:* Holland.
> *Team 1:* Yes! Good work! Excellent! Wow, you sure know stuff. Do you have a B.A. in general arts?

The winner is the team whose members end up feeling the best about themselves.

Other games I have enjoyed but don't have the space to describe include the following:

- Spin the Assault Weapon
- Turkey in the Trousers
- Whose Shoes?
- Simon and Garfunkel Say
- Follow the Leaper
- Thud That Dud Spud, Bud
- Blindman's Buff
- I Spy with My Little Nose
- Hide and Leave
- Hops 'n' Scotch
- Pin the Tail on Someone Tying His Shoes
- Bust a Belly Button
- Kick My Can

HOW TO SAVE FACE

How often has this happened to you? You encounter a friend or acquaintance who inquires about your family and struggle to find a polite way of explaining that your spouse has run off with a stump puller. Here we show you the wrong way and the right way to smooth over these socially awkward moments. And all without telling a single little white lie!

Awkward Situation #1

Incorrect

Friend: "How's that son of yours doing?"
You: "He's in prison for armed robbery."

Correct

Friend: "How's that son of yours doing?"
You: "He's with the government. Full time. Department of correctional services. Got his own office. And they've guaranteed him at least seven years."

Awkward Situation #2

Incorrect

Friend: "How's your wonderful wife?"
You: "She ran off with my best friend."

Correct

Friend: "How's your wonderful wife?"
You: "Great. In all the time I've known her, she hasn't been happier. She's just full of fun and finally enjoying life."

Awkward Situation #3

Incorrect

Friend: "So how are things at work?"
You: "I was fired so they could make a profit."

Correct

Friend: "So how are things at work?"
You: "Great. The place is finally making a profit. And I was the one who made the difference."

Awkward Situation #4

Incorrect

Friend: "You look different. Did you get a haircut?"
You: "No, I put on twenty pounds, went on a nine-week bender, fell down drunk, and broke my nose."

Correct

Friend: "You look different. Did you get a haircut?"
You: "Yep."

Awkward Situation #5

Incorrect

Friend: "How's your father-in-law?"
You: "Nasty, stupid, rude, ignorant, bossy, unclean, overbearing, insensitive, and unpleasant."

Correct

Friend: "How's your father-in-law?"
You: "Same as always."

Awkward Situation #6

Incorrect

Friend: "So what's new with your grandfather?"
You: "He's stone dead."

Correct

Friend: "So what's new with your grandfather?"
You: "Oh, you know . . . he can't complain. He's out of that old folks' home he hated so much. And the kids seem to like him a lot more lately."

THE ADVANTAGES OF BEING UGLY

Over the years I've met a number of good-looking people and a whole lot of ugly ones, and I think the ugly people have more fun. The beautiful ones get people staring at them all the time, and giving them important jobs with responsibility, and trying to have sex with them at various sporting events and hardware conventions. When you're ugly, nobody bothers you like that. And when you're good-looking, everybody expects you to be stupid. Whereas when you're ugly, people assume you're smart, and as long as you don't ever say or do anything, they'll keep that opinion. That's why most politicians are ugly.

The only downside to being unattractive is the "pity factor." I don't want anybody feeling sorry for me because I'm not handsome. I look at it this way: no matter how good you look now, you're going to be ugly someday. Look at anybody over a hundred. That's how we're all going to look eventually. We're all going to be ugly sometime in the future. Those of us who are ugly now are just mature beyond our years.

HOW TO SAVE YOUR MARRIAGE

The secret to a strong marriage is to share each other's interests. Or better still, to have her share your interests. Now, statistics show that a large percentage of women don't enjoy fishing. (And statistically women live longer than men, but I'm sure that's just a coincidence.)

So here are ten sure-fire "lines" that will "lure" your spouse to get "hooked" on fishing. Good luck, "chum."

Most Effective

1) "Did you know that fish oil can remove wrinkles from a person's skin? Scaling as few as five bass can make you look years younger."
2) "There's something really romantic about the sun rising on a lake in the middle of nowhere when it's freezing cold."
3) "Trolling for bass is all the rage in New York."
4) "Why is it that hip waders make a person look fifteen pounds thinner?"

Less Effective

5) "If there are any minnows left over, you can dip them in lacquer and make beautiful earrings out of them."
6) "When I'm fishing, I don't talk."
7) "The kids won't be coming along."

Least Effective

8) "Fishing could save us a bundle of money. I mean, it's free food! All we pay for is the gas, the bait, the beer, the parking, the boat-launching fees, the lures, the rods, and the sunburn cream."
9) "Don't worry about bugs—the bats eat them."
10) "The great thing is you can go to the bathroom right over the side of the boat."

HOW TO GO WEEKEND CAMPING

Step One

Go on Tuesday. Avoid the crowds.

Step Two

You'll need a good excuse to get off work or to escape from your loved ones or any other unpleasant responsibilities. A good way to do that is to put your own obituary in the paper. This will stop people from looking for you—but it only works once.

Step Three

Borrow a tent, bedroll, camp stove, hamper, cooler, and portable TV from a friend you can afford to lose. Heave it all into your vehicle. Back out of your driveway and immediately pull into the passing lane. Press your right foot on the accelerator and your left hand on the horn, and maintain that position until you run out of gas or hit something, which will signify that it's time to start camping.

Step Four

If there are other campers already there, go to the biggest, most tattooed guy and have him throw a beer bottle as far as he can. Make sure you camp beyond that. If you don't feel like pitching your own tent, pretend you're having trouble with it and for sure a liberated woman will stop and do it for you. Exchanging physical work for minor humiliation is an acceptable trade-off.

Step Five

Instead of building a campfire, find a tall, dry tree and ignite it. Not only is this an excellent source of heat and light, but it also will keep away the bugs and people who wear a lot of hairspray, like television evangelists or professional bowlers. For fun, toast up some marshmallows till they're hot and gooey and then drop them on the faces of your sleeping friends. When it's time to put the fire out, beer makes an excellent extinguisher, as long as you drink it first.

Step Six

Unroll your sleeping bag on a soft, dry surface, such as someone else's sleeping bag. When the owner comes looking, say his bag was swiped by the tattooed guy who threw the bottle. Once you're snug in your sleeping bag, make the loudest and most offensive body noises you can. This will send a clear message to the other campers and the animal kingdom that nobody should mess with you, because you're too busy messing with yourself.

Step Seven

On the off chance that you live until morning, get up quietly and collapse everybody else's tents. This will create a certain amount of confusion and even hostility, so none of them will notice you siphoning their gas.

Step Eight

Grab an armful of other people's cookware and hit the road. The disappointment of having to return to your job or family will be offset by the fun of whipping pots and pans at hitchhikers.

Go back to your normal life and count the days until Tuesday.

AN AUTOBIOGRAPHICAL INTERLUDE

T*he Red Green Show* was not my first stab at television. That surprises most people who've seen it. Over the years, I've hosted a large number of outdoors shows and nature films. Here's some of my other work, which you may or may not have seen and/or enjoyed. I have everything I've ever done recorded on tape (mostly Beta and some eight-tracks).

The Lure of Lures (1971–74). Lure-Id Films, Inc. 26 episodes. Every week I talked for a half-hour about fishing lures. My guests included a very young Michelle Pfeiffer. This series can sometimes be seen in reruns after 4 a.m. on small cable channels during thunderstorms.

"Mr. Bait" Commercials (1975–77). I was the official spokesperson for the Mr. Bait Shop in town. I loaned my face and good name to promote their fine line of fishing bait. Most people don't remember seeing me in those commercials—perhaps because my face was somewhat obscured by the giant worm costume.

Run, Kids! It's a Big, Bad Fire! (1978). This was a film I made for the local fire department. It was an educational film warning schoolchildren about the dangers of playing with matches. To save money, we filmed it at my house. Ironically, one of the bright movie lights set fire to a stack of empties and burned the place down. The profits from the film almost covered the $500 deductible on my fire insurance policy.

Let's Fry Something Good (1980–83). Fry Films, Inc. 45 episodes. This was a cooking show I did with my wife, Bernice. Each week she would fry up a different meal—fish, chicken, spaghetti. I would sit on a stool and banter with her and ask questions like "Is that a real apple?" At the end of the show, I would taste what Bernice had prepared and smile at the camera and go "MmmmmmMMM!" (Golly, that was acting.) Series·was cancelled when my cholesterol level surpassed our ratings.

Understanding Computers (1984). An educational TV series about understanding and using your brand-new home computer. I hosted the show and played the part of the viewer—the person who knows nothing about computers. Over the series, I learned all about software and hardware and so on from my tutor—played by my then five-year-old nephew. The show had a good budget, a great time slot, and lots of snazzy special effects. Our only mistake was choosing the Mattel Intellivision as our computer.

Cars and Bikinis (1985). Headlight Productions. Pilot episode only. This was a great idea that never went to series. Kind of like *Baywatch*, but with cars too. Just too ahead of its time.

Explosions! (1986). BoomBoom Films. Pilot episode only. This was an educational series about the history of things blowing up. An unfortunate incident during filming shut the project down. Later, the A&E network bought the idea off me for thirty dollars and retitled it *Brute Force*, and it was a hit. Timing is everything. As we learned during that unfortunate accident during filming.

Buster and the Fat Man (1987–88). Thriller Productions. (Made for the Canadian cable TV channel Mystery Movies of the Week.) I moved behind the camera to try my hand at writing, directing, producing, set designing, costume designing, lighting, gripping, publicizing, and editing. Concept: a couple of wisecracking detectives walk a fine line between danger and comedy and justice. The Fat Man is an ex-cop and circus sword swallower. Buster is a former con, born in England, raised by wolves, now rebuilding his life. I reused a lot of footage from *Explosions!* and *Cars and Bikinis*. It was a great concept, lots of fun, but making the two lead characters Siamese twins was, in hindsight, a mistake. The titles of the four movies are *Dial 911 for Murder*; *Love, Larceny, and Larry*; *The Maltese Possum*; and *Murder Most Lousy*. These movies can still be seen in reruns at my house when there's nothing else on and I'm feeling sorry for myself.

Acid Rain! What Acid Rain? (1988). The Association of Canadian Mining Corporations. 22 minutes. Another educational film I made on behalf of some very big companies. During filming, I learned a whole bunch of stuff about the environment I didn't know before. The upbeat message of this film is that Mother Nature is a lot more resilient than we think.

HOW TO CREATE THREE CHARMING DECORATOR ACCENTS FROM STUFF YOU'D NORMALLY THROW OUT

Bowling Ball Flowerpot

Got an old bowling ball that's dented or broken or always flies into the gutter for some reason? Don't toss it. Turn it into a lovely ebony flower holder.

How? Clamp the ball in a large vise so the finger holes face down. Sand the top side of the ball until it's somewhat flat. Remove from vise. Turn the ball over so it rests on its flat surface. Put flowers in the finger holes. (Drill more holes for a fuller bouquet.)

Baby Playpen Wine Rack

Have your babies grown up and reached drinking age? Don't throw out their old playpen, because your kids'll probably get married, have nine kids of their own, become unemployed, and announce they're moving back into your home.

If you get lucky and they don't move back, why not turn that playpen into a lovely wine rack? After all, with the kids gone, you can afford some nice wine.

How? Disassemble the playpen, making sure not to wreck the four sides. Take two sides and lay one on top of the other, at right angles, so that the posts form a cross pattern. Screw, nail, glue, or—better still—duct-tape the two sides together. Repeat with the remaining two sides. Join them with short lengths of wood. And you've got a wine rack! Now stock it with baby bottles filled with homemade beer. Then when you're thirsty, grab a bottle and suck on the nipple. Is that heaven or what?

Steam Rad Circus Calliope

When you convert your house from hot-water radiators to forced-air gas, save a couple of those old iron rads. They'll make a great steam calliope, like the ones the old circuses used to have before they all went bankrupt.

How? I'm not sure. Our house has electric baseboard heaters. But it shouldn't be hard.

THE JOY OF MIDDLE AGE

I want to talk to all you middle-aged guys about the fading urges, the sense that you are maybe not the passionate lover you once were—at least the way you tell it.

First of all, the fact that you've changed from a young stag who is eager to rut into an old drag who's stuck in a rut is a good thing. There is less chance you'll become a father at a time when you no longer have the patience or the energy or the brain power to, say, help with homework.

Another upside to the loss of your sex drive is that once or twice a week, for a few fleeting minutes, you'll actually be able to concentrate on other stuff, like, say, your job.

So accept the declining desire. Your wife is probably just as happy to read in bed and you get to watch all the hockey games, even if there's overtime.

THE BIG CHILL

I was kind of a rebellious teenager, looking to lash out against authority. And I could always find someone willing to take me on. Nowadays, I walk away from confrontational people and spend my time with friends.

I recommend that instead of looking for people to hit, we all start looking for people to hug. But not in a subway full of strangers. I'll never make that mistake again.

HOW STRONG IS YOUR MARRIAGE?

Find out with this quiz. The questions apply to both men and women. You and your significant other should answer these questions honestly and openly. Just never, ever show each other your answers.

1) My marriage is more important to me than:
   a) my work
   b) my weekend
   c) my own chances for long-term happiness

2) When I have a serious problem, I know I can count on my spouse to:
   a) be there for me
   b) laugh at me
   c) be the source of it all
   d) blab it to all his/her friends

3) My spouse and I laugh at the same things:
   a) usually
   b) rarely
   c) only if they happen to me

4) I would say that my spouse feels like our sex life is:
   a) exciting
   b) adequate
   c) distracting
   d) a vague memory

5) I think it's important for a couple to share the same:
   a) values
   b) religious beliefs

c) cutlery

d) undershorts

6) My spouse buys special fancy silk undergarments for me to wear:

a) now and then

b) all the time

c) when my hernia flares up

7) On our honeymoon, my spouse and I discovered:

a) how much we love each other

b) how much we love hot tubs

c) how much we love all the great movies on the hotel's pay TV

8) As a couple, we try to set aside quality time for each other:

a) at least twice a day

b) at least once a week

c) during commercials

9) The famous couple we are most like is:

a) Romeo and Juliet

b) Sonny and Cher

c) Brad and Angelina

d) the *Bismarck* and the *Hood*

10) If my spouse and I had to do it all over again, knowing what we know now:

a) we would get married again

b) we would live together first

c) I'd kill myself

d) I'd kill him/her

e) I'd hold out for a bigger dowry

f) I'd hold out for a bigger everything

g) I'd hold out

HOW TO ANSWER WHEN SHE ASKS THE "AM I FAT?" QUESTION

There are certain times when the woman in your life will ask you a question and you won't have time to think about your answer. This is the worst one.

You're not going to say yes unless you have a death wish, but you have to say no the right way or this conversation will go into triple overtime. Just say no. Right away. As soon as she asks. Just say no. Just like that. No pause. No thinking it over. No saying, "Well . . . no, not really."

But don't go too far the other way either. You can't say, "What, you? Fat? Ha! Get serious. Don't make me laugh! Tell me another one! Sure, all your friends are fat, and so are your sisters, but not you! No way! You're like an underfed chicken. It's sickening how thin you are." Because as I believe Shakespeare said, "Methinks the lady doth process too much."

So when she asks, "Am I fat?" just say no and then ask her to go out for dinner. That way you'll look like a hero, and since she's worried about her weight, she'll probably refuse the invitation. It's a win-win.

THE OVER-FIFTIES: A WORD

I want to talk to you middle-aged guys about job security. I've had a few jobs myself over the years, so I know the pink-slip warning signs. If you skip off work for a day and nobody notices, that's a bad sign. Or your boss keeps showing new employees around your office and asking them, "What about here?" That's not good. Or you take a one-week holiday and they replace you with a twelve-year-old kid who doesn't speak English. Then when you return, he gets a going-away party where everybody cries. And your boss writes down the kid's home phone number.

If this sounds familiar to you, there are several steps you can take to prepare for the inevitable disaster.

Step one: Marry someone who has a job.

Step two: Get on first-name terms with everybody at the employment insurance place.

But most of all, don't get down on yourself. Try to look on the bright side of being unemployed. Your time's your own. No traffic problems—you wake up in the morning and you're there.

When I was between jobs, from early June of 1982 to late August of 1989, I managed to keep my head up. A lot of people are working hard making money doing something they don't enjoy (work), whereas you're taking it easy making zip doing something you love (nothing). It's not such a bad trade-off.

TIPS FOR INVESTORS

Thinking of investing in the stock market? Or mutual funds? Or land in Florida? Here are some things to look for and some things to avoid in any opportunity.

Good Signs

- Your investment is insured.
- The investment company is using its own letterhead, not stationery from a local motel.

- other investors include large companies, well-known business figures, and members of organized crime.
- The mutual fund never invests in Canadian-made movies or sitcoms.

Bad Signs

- The salesman only lets you read every other page of the documents you have to sign.
- The salesman wears a paper bag on his head.
- The fine print on the contract is in a foreign language.
- Your investment counsellor drives a pink Cadillac with huge fuzzy dice, a fun fur interior, and the licence plate "TUFF GUY."
- The head of the fund has to borrow cab fare to get home.
- They promise a million percent annual profit on your investment.

IN PRAISE OF OLDER MOWERS

When I was a kid, we had an old pull-start lawn mower. You'd tie a knot in one end of a rope and hook that into the hub on top, and then give it a good yank. Sometimes, if your brother was standing too close, the knotted end of the rope would whip out and nail him in the groinal area. That was always good for a laugh. Eventually the knot would break off and you'd have to tie another and then another, and in time, the rope got too short to use. So you'd go to the hardware store and buy a new piece and start the process all over again. It was inconvenient and sometimes irritating, but on the other hand, you always knew how to fix the problem, and that made you feel strong and in control.

Now, of course, we all have electric-start riding mowers. That's progress. They're way easier to start and they do a better, faster cutting job. The downside is that when something goes wrong you have no idea how to fix it, and that makes you feel weak and out of control. Plus, when you nail your brother in the groinal area with one of those babies, it can be serious.

HER CAR, YOUR FAULT

She scrimped and saved her own money for two years to buy that car. She did not give you permission to drive it. But you just had to go behind her back and take it for a drive anyway, didn't you? And you just had to go to a lumberyard and pick up two sheets of drywall and then try to jam them into that tiny little hatchback. And you just had to rip the upholstery on the roof. Now what are you going to tell her? Well, you're not going to tell her anything. Not yet. First you have to ditch the drywall, hop back in the car, and go pick up her three nephews. Yes, those three rotten, destructive children of Satan. Take them out somewhere for ice cream and pop and chocolate. Lots of chocolate. And make sure they spend at least an hour in her car. By the time those hyenas are done, your rip on the roof liner's going to look like an afterthought. That'll get you off the hook. How can she get mad at you? You were just trying to give her nephews a treat. It's not your fault they're destructive, nasty little sociopaths. They're family.

TEN SIGNS THAT YOU MIGHT BE NON-COMMUNICATIVE

1) When you phone somebody, you're hoping to get his voicemail.
2) You never ask anyone a question because you have no interest in her answer.
3) When you have a passenger in your car, you turn the radio up as loud as it will go.
4) You spend a lot of time alone in the garage.
5) When you have something to say, you speak loudly without taking a pause and then quickly exit the room.
6) Email is your favourite method of communication because you can say whatever you want without interruption and then delete the reply without reading it.
7) Instead of saying "Good morning" when you come upon someone you know walking in the street, you pretend to see something important in the distance and start running toward it.
8) Your office phone has been set on voicemail since 1991.
9) On the rare occasion when you send greeting cards, you don't sign them.
10) You wear headphones that aren't plugged into anything.

WHY MEN WON'T ASK FOR DIRECTIONS

I need to talk to all you ladies out there to help you understand why we men do the things we do. For example, why won't we stop and ask for directions when we're lost? It all comes down to pride. We're out there driving around in our own vehicle, burning gas, wearing sunglasses, looking good. People who see us driving by would never guess that we have no idea where we are. And we don't want to tell them.

A man doesn't enjoy the thought of going up to total strangers and saying, "You may not know this, but I'm a moron." In contrast, the woman he's travelling with is often eager to share this knowledge with the world. It somehow eases her burden.

To a woman, getting lost on a trip is a blameless act of nature; to a man, it's a personal failure. He knew where he was when he left home, but he doesn't know where he is now. Somewhere along the way, he crossed the line from the world he knows into the world he doesn't know. This is how he felt when he got married or had kids. If he admits he's lost in the car, he'll have to admit that he's lost everywhere, and that's way too much to ask. So just bite your tongue and circle the block a few more times. Men aren't lost—they just go the long way round.

THE SEVEN STAGES OF PARKING

What are we all looking for as we drive down the highway of life? A decent place to park.

Stage One

You're a kid. All you have to park is your butt.

Stage Two

You're a teenager and you park with a girl who has a good chance of becoming your future wife.

Stage Three

You're married with kids and are parking a minivan at the McDonald's with the play area.

Stage Four

The kids are grown and working at McDonald's. You've got a sports car and are caught parking with a girl who has no chance of becoming your future wife. This leads immediately to . . .

Stage Five

You're parking in the garage, where you're also living for a while.

Stage Six

You're old—no car, no licence, no parking spot.

Stage Seven

You're parked. Permanently. In your own space. Even has your name over it.

AN EXTRAORDINARY MAN

I was watching one of those biography shows on television this week, and they called this particular guy an "extraordinary man." I was intimidated. But on the other hand, my wife says being a man isn't a particularly high calling. So being an "extraordinary" one might be even worse.

Let's break the word down: "extra"—which means superfluous, waste, one too many (I've been there)—and "ordinary"—which means common, average, nothing special. When you put them together, you get "extraordinary," which must mean being completely average in a totally superfluous way.

So I've decided that I am extraordinary too. And so are most of my friends. I'm just amazed that somebody like me became the subject of a television show.

HOW TO TELL WHEN A MAN IS CLUELESS

Attention ladies—men are drawn to machines like moths to a flame. Especially if the machine is broken. However, when a woman has a broken machine, the last thing she needs is an interfering guy who has no idea what he's doing. It's fine if that guy is her husband or her neighbour, because then she knows he's an idiot and can keep him away. But with strangers, it can be hard to tell. So here are some signs that indicate this guy has no idea what he's doing:

- He stares at the machine for more than ten minutes without moving or speaking.
- He tells you to shut the machine off.
- He finds a control and turns it a little and waits. Then he turns it a lot and waits. Then he turns it back to its original position.
- He burns himself on something and pretends it never happened.
- He sprays the entire machine and surrounding area with oil.
- He hides his tool box.

- As soon as another man arrives on the scene, he backs away just far enough that he regresses from partici-pant to observer.

A WORD TO YOUNG DRIVERS

I know that we have a lot of young people out there reading this book as some sort of punishment, so here are a few tips on driving from someone a little older who's been down the road a time or two.

Let's say you've just got your driver's licence and you're excited as heck about that, and the next thing you know, you've stolen a car. And naturally you go over to your high school to do a little showing off—doing doughnuts and figure eights in the flower-beds, up on two wheels and then in through the front doors so you can peel rubber up and down the halls. I know that may sound like a lot of fun, but please play it smart: wear your seat belt.

ANOTHER WORD TO YOUNG DRIVERS

I know a lot of you teenagers would kill to have your own car, but I'm hoping that won't be necessary. Cheap cars are always available through one of those drug lord used car dealers or the police, or if that fails, just call up the hospital and see if anybody who's in intensive care would like to sell their car. You'll find something—just as long as you're not picky about the make or the colour or the stains on the seats. Once you get the car, fill out the insurance form and list your grandmother as principal driver. Get yourself a part-time job at the gas station and take a couple of gallons of your work home with you every night. Make friends with one of the ratchetheads in auto shop and date a girl with money and you'll have the best summer of your life. And you'll have some great stories to tell the judge in traffic court.

TATTOOS: A PERMANENTLY STUPID IDEA

Young people, it's me again. I know a lot of you feel you have to rebel and be obnoxious and embarrass your parents in restaurants, but that's just a normal part of growing up and finding your place in the world, especially when your parents throw you out. Whereas getting a tattoo is stupid.

Now, I don't mean one of those temporary transfer dealies in the box of Crunchie Critters. I'm talking about a carnival-booth, skin-carved, sober-up-and-scream-about-it tattoo. A tattoo is basically a liquid sliver. And the liquid is permanent ink. Getting a tattoo is like sucking on a pen with your whole body.

And it's painful. There are only two things more painful than getting a tattoo: getting two tattoos, and getting either of them removed. Maybe there's some appeal in getting "Guns N' Roses" tattooed on your butt, but sixty years from now, in the middle of your hemorrhoid operation, you're going to find out why it's not a good idea to get your surgeon laughing.

HOW TO TELL WHEN YOU'RE BEING OBNOXIOUS

Sometimes when a man reaches middle age, he gets a little full of himself. Maybe he's been reasonably successful at work, has a nice home and family, and hasn't raised any convicted felons, so he starts thinking that he knows it all. This ticks off everyone around him, and ironically, he's the last one to notice. So watch for the following signs that indicate you're getting obnoxious:

- People at work volunteer you for a climb of Mount Everest.
- When you talk to the neighbours they run away, pretending to hear their phones ring.
- On Valentine's Day, you're given a box of prunes.
- When the two of you travel, your wife insists that you go on separate planes.
- The other guys in your carpool kick the muffler off your car so they can't hear what you're saying.
- Your best friend works for Amway but has never tried to sell you anything.
- When the firemen arrive, the first thing they do is hose you down.
- Whenever you talk at a party, your wife sits behind you shaking her head.

DRIVING WITH ATTITUDE

Just as your clothes and your grooming and your gun collection define who you are, so does your driving. The meek shall inherit the slow lane. Drive with attitude.

Peeling Rubber

Nothing says "man on the go" like sixty feet of blue smoke and a neighbourhood-piercing squeal. Sure, it cuts down on tread life, but hey, there's a lot of rubber on those tires and you don't know how long you'll be driving—what with the price of gas and the licence suspensions.

If your car doesn't have the power to spin the tires, crimp the rear brake lines and rev her up with your foot on the brake pedal. The front wheels will hold her back and the back tires will be screaming like a banshee. (Not recommended for front-wheel-drive vehicles.)

Laying a black streak across the road is more than just decorative—you can use peeling rubber to intimidate other motorists. When you're at a red light, step on the brake (see above) and rev the engine until the tachometer needle moves as far as it can in a clockwise direction, preferably disappearing below the bottom edge of the control panel. Then jerk your foot off the clutch so that it pops up. Hang on to the steering wheel and hold your breath until the smell dies down, just as you do in your normal daily activities. Release the brake and try to stay on the road. Don't worry about other drivers—they usually get out of the way. Just another upside when you're driving with attitude.

Speeding

Speeding is a natural phenomenon. People who aren't sure where they're going must speed to arrive on time. Driving is an entrepreneurial process, full of negotiation and strategic positioning, with no limits. Especially not speed limits. Speed limits are the result of a lack of speeders. If everybody speeds, the government will raise the limit. Remember how the government got rid of prohibition and the death penalty? And how much that helped your family? Every time you get a speeding ticket, your fellow drivers are letting you down. They need to tap into that "pedal to the metal" attitude. You'll never hit a car you've already passed, so put the hammer down. And if you get caught, I never heard of you.

Tailgating

It's a natural progression from speeding to the subject of tailgating. There is no better way to inform another driver that he's not going fast enough and has become a hazard to traffic than for you to rest your hood ornament up against his trunk lid. To tailgate properly, you should be able to read all the dials on the other guy's dashboard. The sweat on the back of his neck is another sign that you're close enough.

After various turn signals and hand signals, he should pull over and let you pass, but even if he doesn't, his slipstream is helping your gas mileage, and you can turn off your own headlights and just use his. The only way you can have an accident is if you're not following closely enough. As long as you're resting against him, you can't possibly collide with him.

Merging

Occasionally a highway is under construction or there's been an accident or the police are pulling cars over because they can, and this often means that two lanes of traffic have to merge into one. Some drivers believe this should be done in a fair, orderly way, but who has that kind of time? Instead, cruise onto the shoulder and rocket past all the cars, and then cut in front of somebody, and then wave thanks. Now and then, you'll find yourself embroiled in a game of chicken, where the guy you're trying to cut off recklessly speeds up so you can't get in. In this situation, always try to cut off a car that's more valuable than yours. And better maintained. If you're a lodge member, you should have plenty of choices.

Focusing on Driving

The most effective way to drive with attitude is to focus all your concentration on the three basic fundamentals: the gas, the brakes, and the steering. Don't let yourself get distracted by the peripheral controls, like the horn, the windshield wipers, the lights, and the turn signals. Keep them guessing. In the Information Age, the more data you keep to yourself, the more power you have. So drive fast, drive hard, and always carry your insurance agent's home number.

HOW TO GET EVEN

- When your boss criticizes you in front of your fellow workers, yell back that you know what he's up to but you don't find him even remotely attractive.
- When you know your teenage son is going to use your car, empty the gas tank and fill the back seat with fast food packages.
- Buy three sets of golf clubs and keep them together so they can all see that you don't need to keep using ones that misbehave.
- While the cop is writing out your ticket, draw an unflattering sketch of him and hand it to him when he's done.

YOU SHOULD BE COMMITTED

Last week I met a guy who is very socially active. He's involved with this and that and the other, and he doesn't seem to get much out of any of them. That's because he's involved in so many things, he doesn't have time to be committed to any. There's a big difference between being involved and being committed. It's like bacon and eggs: the chicken is involved, but the pig is committed.

You must make a commitment. Marriage is the most popular one, but there are others: spending two months' salary on golf clubs, feeding a stray cat, getting your football team's logo tattooed on your forehead, buying the first round, being the first one in the hot tub to remove his bathing suit (unless you're alone or immediately become that way). So if you're not getting enough out of life, don't do more. Instead, do less but do it harder.

GETTING SHORT WITH TALL GUYS

I'm not a tall person. Just barely average height, actually. So I've always had tall guys around me—taking charge, attracting women, helping me find my car in a crowded parking lot, that kind of thing. I always feel somehow disadvantaged around tall guys, so I'd like to use this space for a little "get even" time.

I know the tall guys won't listen, but maybe you normal people will. First of all, tall guys are here to mate with tall women and have tall children to ensure the future of the NBA. To be a short guy going out with a tall girl takes a special kind of man who is very well adjusted and doesn't have a bald spot. Short guys want to go out with short girls. Short girls are hard to find, and short, attractive girls are a small percentage of that select group. So when a tall guy starts dating an attractive short girl, all the laws of nature are at risk. Tall guys should not be allowed to go out with short girls. They should have a sign on their tie saying, "You must be this tall to go on this ride."

And don't be fooled, ladies. Just because a guy is tall that doesn't mean he's smart. His brain has a lot of heavy work to do: moving that huge body around without falling over, ducking under doorways, and avoiding lightning. A short guy's brain can think about other things—like you. Short guys make better lovers. They're more responsive, more attentive, more grateful. And they won't get in your way, personally or professionally. With a short guy, you can have your ear to the ground and still maintain eye contact.

TEN SIGNS YOU ARE TAKING EACH OTHER FOR GRANTED

1) In a group photo taken recently, you have trouble picking out your wife.
2) You drive in the car for three hours without speaking, and that's fine with her.
3) The cancellation of *Wheel of Fortune* would create a depressing void in both of your lives.
4) For your anniversary, you bought her the exact same ball cap you bought her last year. And she didn't notice.
5) Your wife discusses your medical condition with her friends while you're present and then wants you to show them the scar.
6) You can use your meals as a calendar: meat loaf is Monday, chicken is Tuesday, McDonald's is payday . . .
7) A sit-down dinner at your house involves TV trays.
8) On a night when you're working late, you call home to tell her and that makes her suspicious.
9) Neither of you goes to bed until you're really, really tired.
10) Your wife bought matching shirts so you could be each other once in a while.

KEEPING THE MAGIC ALIVE

If you're a married man and you're hoping to stay that way, I think it's a good idea to do everything you can to maintain your value in your wife's eyes. You should treat yourself the way you would a car you plan to keep for a long time. Wash and wax as often as you can. Change the oil once a month. No quick starts or stops. And keep the mileage down.

That'll take care of your physical appearance, but to get to the heart and mind of a woman, you need to have a little mystique working for you. Instead of actually having an affair, just pretend you are. Have women call you at home and then hang up when your wife answers. Throw a tube of passion pink lipstick into your glove compartment. Speak French in your sleep. Life is an auction, and nothing increases the value of an item more than the fear that someone else is bidding. And when your wife finds out that you're actually not cheating on her, she'll have a huge victory celebration and you'll be the guest of honour. Rest up.

GUILTY BY ASSOCIATION

I saw an article in a movie magazine about an aging actress, and it included some pictures of her in her personal life with her husband. He isn't a show biz guy. He made his money in shoe stores or something. And that may be what created the problem. Because he's not an entertainer, he doesn't really care what he looks like. At the very least, it's okay for him to look old. In contrast, she's had more corrective surgery than Joe Namath's knees. So when you see them together, you think, "Why would a young, good-looking woman like her be with an old dog like him? And how can her son possibly be older than she is?" I guess for cosmetic surgery to work properly, everybody in your family has to agree to have it done. All it takes is one wrinkled younger sister and your cover is blown.

WHAT TO DO WHEN YOUR CAR WON'T START

You don't have to be a licensed mechanic to have a car that won't start. Here are some simple steps that will save you money by preventing you from going to the mall.

Step One: Ignition Check

- Is the key in the ignition?
- Is it the car key?
- Are you turning it the right way?
- Does the motor turn over?
- Do you know what "turn over" means? (You married guys do.)
- If the motor doesn't turn over, check the battery. Wipe off the top of the battery and lay your tongue across both terminals. Check your watch. If you blacked out for more than an hour, the battery is fine.
- Remove a spark plug for a random test. Slide your earlobe into the spark plug gap and have a friend crank the starter. If it works, you should now have a pierced ear.
- When you're satisfied that the ignition is okay, move on to the fuel check.

Step Two: Fuel Check

- Does the fuel gauge show there's gas?
- Does the fuel gauge work?

- Is there a fuel gauge?
- Have you ever looked at the fuel gauge before?
- Did your teenager borrow the vehicle and promise, swear, and vow on his honour to gas it up?
- Remove the gas cap. Do you see gas?
- Do you smell gas?
- Do you taste gas?
- Are you standing in gas?
- If you enjoy travelling, hold a match up to the gas filler tube.
- Disconnect the outlet tube from the fuel pump. It's probably a metric fitting, so you may as well snip her off with side cutters. Look down the end of the tube while a friend cranks the motor. If you detect a fair amount of excess gas in your eye, the fuel pump is fine. Reconnect the tube with duct tape.
- Find every adjusting screw on the carburetor and turn them all the way in one direction. Try the engine. Now turn them all the way in the other direction. Try the engine again. Now set them all roughly somewhere in the middle.
- The automatic choke mechanism can rarely be fixed, so whack it a few times with a hammer just for fun.
- Now that you've ruled out ignition or fuel problems, move on to alternative starting techniques.

Step Three: Alternative Starting Techniques

For an older car that has never had a tune-up or an oil change or a tank of brand-name gas, a car battery may not have enough power. To rectify this problem, attach battery cables to both terminals. Run the cables into the house and plug them into the stove circuit. Set your rad to 425 degrees Fahrenheit, and your engine should be done in about an hour. Baste lightly. Serves six anxious passengers.

Maybe the starting motor doesn't turn the engine over fast enough. If so, take your car to the top of a big hill (better still, always remember to park at the top of a big hill), then turn on the ignition and roll it down. Pop the clutch often and with attitude. If the car won't start, try rolling it backwards down the hill. If that doesn't work, try rolling it sideways into a ravine.

Bring a crushed car home from the auto wrecker. Park it in front of your car and say, "This could be you." If a car won't start with threats, it's finished. But you still deserve some satisfaction.

Step Four: Satisfaction

A Saturday afternoon with a ten-pound sledgehammer can really ease the frustration of a car that refuses to start. And when you've had your fill from every conceivable angle, hose the vehicle down with barbecue starter and give it a Viking funeral. A stunning milestone in the battle of man against machine.

Step Five: Afterthought

Make sure it's your car.

HOW TO IMPROVE YOUR GAS MILEAGE

Ever since the oil crisis in the mid-seventies, people have been concerned about gas mileage. Here are a few tips that you won't get from the EPA, the NRA, or the CIA.

Save Money on Gas

An average tank of gas costs $530. An average gas syphon costs $7.95. Do the math.

Hang out at self-serve stations with a gas can. While a guy is going up to pay, squeeze yourself a can out of his pump.

Conserve Gas

- Magnetize your front bumper. Pull onto the highway and tailgate. Shut your engine off. Don't start your car until you come to your exit. You'll save a fortune.
- Don't go anywhere that isn't downhill. This means you'll have to come home by a different route. And it won't be your home. But that may not be a bad thing.
- Turn the engine off every time you're coasting or stopped. (Make sure you have a good battery.)
- Pretend you don't have a good battery and ask people to push-start you. Just keep yelling, "Almost! Almost! A bit faster!" And let them push you all the way to the mall. If they complain, point out how good an aerobic workout they've just had without having to pay expensive membership fees to a health club.
- Carpool to work and be "sick" whenever it's your turn.
- Take the energy-saver nozzle off your bathroom showerhead and splice it onto your gas line. This will restrict the amount of gas that flows to the engine. (Don't try to pass on a hill.)
- If you have an enormous, gas-guzzling North American car, put it in Neutral and tow it behind a hybrid.
- An engine uses very little gas when idling. Disconnect the gas pedal and idle everywhere. It's a great way to avoid high-speed accidents and to get attention from other drivers.

- When driving into the wind, remove things that cause drag, like hood ornaments and side-view mirrors. When driving with the wind at your back, open your doors and trunk so they'll act like sails.
- Experiment with alternative fuels such as methane, propane, rubbing alcohol, shoe polish, and road tar.
- If you have teenage drivers, you can limit the amount of gas they use by not putting any in.
- You can reduce your own gas consumption by having your licence suspended.

Lower Your Car's Curb Weight

- Remove anything you don't really use. Start with the things you use the least: turn signals, curb feelers, spare tire, jack, passenger seat, mirrors, lights, gauges, hood, trunk lid, fuzzy dice, passengers, little ceramic doggie with the bobbing head.
- Clean your car. I removed over two hundred pounds of old candy wrappers, ripped maps, coffee cups, etc., from under the driver's seat of the Possum van. I would have got more out, but I use the bottom layers as my floor.
- Inflate the tires with hydrogen. (Not recommended for fire trucks.)
- Do not maintain the finish on your car. Rust is lighter than metal.
- Oil the body. If oil reduces the friction inside the engine, why not reduce the friction on the outside? Aerodynamics is an important component of speed. That's why fat people can't run.
- The most efficient body style is small in the front and big in the back, which pretty much describes most of the lodge members and their wives. To get the front

end low, try wedging your car under a tractor-trailer at forty miles an hour. To get the back end high, wedge the trunk lid open with a manure shovel. (Leave some manure on it to prevent tailgating.)

· Remove anything on your car that blocks the flow of air: door handles, party streamers, animal carcasses.

· Make your car smooth. Lather it up with car wash soap and then shave it. Remove excess lather with a hot towel and then slap on a polymer-based skin bracer. Once a week should do it, but Italian cars may have to shave more often.

HOW TO HITCHHIKE

You never know what the highway of life will throw at you. Whether you've run out of gas or been run out of town, at some point you're going to have to hitchhike. Here are a few pointers:

Try to look good. Comb your hair, hide the rips in your clothing with your hands, and tuck your beard inside your lips. If you haven't bathed in recent memory, rub yourself down with mint leaves found growing along the side of the road. But don't confuse the mint plant with poison ivy. Nobody will stop for a hitchhiker who is wildly scratching himself. That's the voice of experience.

Try to look friendly. Give oncoming cars a big smile. Show your teeth if they're handy. If you feel like waving, remember to unclench your fist first. And use at least two fingers. If you're a guy, don't try to attract cars by showing cleavage. (If you do, any cars that stop are not ones you should be getting into.) When a driver passes you by, don't start swearing at him and flipping him the bird, unless you're sure the next driver can't see you. The image you want to project is that of a friendly, interesting, unarmed passenger looking for a driver who likes people, light contemporary rock, and long drives in the country.

Be aware that drivers are turned off by little things, such as if your hair is one amorphous blob rather than individual strands, if you're carrying automatic weapons, if you have steam or liquid coming out of your backpack, if your ankles are shackled, if your chainsaw is running, if your pants are in a nearby tree, if a nearby tree is now in your pants. Again, trust me on this: you'll wait days for a ride.

You need the sympathy rather than the contempt of drivers, so try to look like you're temporarily out of luck, rather than permanently out of alternatives. Carrying an empty gas can is good because it implies you have a car somewhere. A shirt and tie suggests that hitchhiking was an unplanned exercise. When drivers approach, shrug your shoulders like "Can you believe this?" They just might.

It's good to carry a sign that clearly defines your destination. And it should be somewhere on earth. Your sign should be neat, and not written in blood or lipstick. It shouldn't say "I'm going out west, where I belong," unless you're Wilbert Harrison. If you're going to Las Vegas, have the sign say "Las Vegas," rather than "Someplace where prostitution is legal." Otherwise, drivers won't pick you up because they'll assume you're a politician.

Hold your arm straight out like you're proud of it. And have your thumb pointing up. That's important. A thumb pointing down can be taken as a comment on a person's car. If the roadside is narrow, don't be too proud to pull your arm in as cars go by. Very few thumbs can stand even a low-speed automotive collision.

Generally, hitchhikers who expect people to give them a ride really should stop beating, robbing, and killing those people. I'm sure it's a case where the few are spoiling it for the many, but until hitchhikers have a formal organization with a clear code of conduct and a meaningful lobbyist in the seat of government, it will continue to be one of the least reliable forms of transportation, just ahead of the Ford Pinto.

ATTENTION, SHOPPERS

I heard a warning the other day about those Waterpik things people use to blast water between their teeth. The message was not to use the device on my eyes. I had several reactions to that statement. The first one was "Okay, don't squirt a needle of pressurized water into my eye area. That makes sense." My second reaction was "Holy cow, they think I'm a moron. They think that if they don't warn me, I'm going to fire this thing up and try to hose down my retinas." That insulted me. My third and final reaction was acceptance. Acceptance of the idea that protecting people from themselves is never a bad thing, and usually not unnecessary. Seat belts and airbags and warning buzzers and smoke detectors and railings and padded rooms are all there for a reason. Besides, having someone assume you're a moron is not a new experience for most married men.

THE BELL CURVE AND YOU

I'm not exactly sure when I first found out about the bell curve. It was high school, in either physics or math class. It had to do with averaging exam results so that a small number of people at the bottom failed, a small number of people at the top got really high marks, and the bulk of us fell in between, in the big bulge part of the bell curve. In the naiveté of my youth, I thought that was pretty much it for the bell curve. But I've aged a lot since then. I've been able to apply the bell curve to almost every aspect of my life.

In my job, I've learned not to be so bad that I'm at the bottom and get fired, or to be so good that I'm at the top and get blamed. In my personal appearance, I've learned to strive for a midpoint between Regis Philbin and Charlie Sheen. The same with my weight, fitness level, and general behavioural patterns—never good enough for the Nobel Prize, but never bad enough for long-term incarceration.

I believe that true happiness lies at the centre of the bell curve. If you look around your social circle and decide that you're at the bottom end of the bell curve, then you'd better start bringing in people who are actually worse than you, to improve your own position. That's what they do in most of the major corporations and political parties.

HOW TO PREPARE FOR OLD AGE

With luck, we all get old. But you need to be doing things now—while you still have your faculties—that will make your old age as enjoyable as possible. I'm sure you'll be able to come up with ideas yourselves, but here are a few to get you started:

- Get your praying in now, while your knees are still good.
- Make an appointment to have a vasectomy on your ninetieth birthday.
- Buy trophies at garage sales and scatter them all over your house.
- Make up incredible stories about your life. Nobody's going to listen to you anyway, so you might as well have the fun of lying.
- Find things that interest and excite you and stare at them for hours. That way, when you're on your death-bed and your whole life flashes before you, it'll be easier to pay attention.
- When you die, leave everything to your deceased parents—one last shot at screwing up the lawyers.

LESS REALLY IS MORE

I went shopping for some new pants last week. I hadn't measured my waist in a while, but I knew there'd been growth in that area, because more parts of the chair rub against my sides and back. So I grabbed a few pairs to try on, ranging in size from 40 to 44. Well, holy cow, they were all too big. And I mean way too big. I ended up with a size 34. Size 34! I wore a size 34 when I was in high school. I'm doing fine. I'm in shape.

It just so happens I still have a pair of pants from high school up in the attic, so I went up to try them on. It didn't go well. I'm not sure if I could have done up the waist or not, since I couldn't get the pants past the mid-thigh region. Could these pants—these tuxedo pants that haven't been washed ever and haven't been to the cleaners since I spilled that Baby Duck at the prom—have shrunk in the attic? No.

I think we all know the horrible truth: they've changed the sizes. I don't have to take a size 42 because a size 34 is a size 42. But not for all pants. Not for young pants like the ones your kids wear. No, these pants I just bought are old-guy-big-butt pants. They size them liberally because guys don't need another reason not to buy clothes. Especially old guys. With big butts.

WHY BRITISH CARS SUCK

I have personally experienced a long line of British cars. The Morris Minor. The Austin 7. The Vauxhall. The Standard Vanguard. And who can forget the Hillman Minx, no matter how hard they try? These cars have all been various levels of disaster. Although Rolls-Royce and Bentley make arguably the best cars in the world, the rest of the British automotive lineup is pretty pathetic. If you were grading British cars, there'd be a few A students with rich parents and a lot of dropouts, drop-offs, and drop-aparts.

The Longest Journey Begins With the Car Starting

Most British cars won't start in North America. It's too cold or too hot or too dry or too windy or too stressful or too provincial. The British just don't build cars for our climate. The battery is about the size of a pound of butter, so you have only a few chances to get it going. Most people can't start their British cars and so don't show up for work. In Britain, unions are powerful. Is this a coincidence?

Where There's Smoke, There's a British Car

That cloud of blue smoke you see billowing out of that tiny British exhaust pipe is burnt oil. In North America, the philosophy is to burn gas and lubricate with oil. In Britain, they burn oil and lubricate with beer. And you can tell by the smell of the blue smoke that oil is not a clean-burning fuel. The problem stems from the looseness of the engine parts. The pistons flop around in the cylinders and the valves flop around in the guides and the oil flops all over everything. Maybe the price of gas is so high that the British have simply given up and switched to oil, or maybe it's the only way to trace a getaway car when your police officers are unarmed and on bicycles and all named Bobby.

"Minor" Is Right

The bodies are tiny. But the windows are normal-sized. From a distance they look like a cartoon of a car; Woody Woodpecker would not look out of place behind the steering wheel. British cars are small because they're made for short, narrow roads with quaint hamlets every three miles. Our highways are often three thousand miles long, and most of the drivers have never seen *Hamlet*.

A little Morris Minor winding out at a top-end speed of sixty-three miles an hour with a vapour trail of blue smoke is not going to fare well between a couple of tractor-trailers with pup trailers jammed full of livestock. It's a tiny car with tiny lights whizzing along on tiny tires. Those tires would look oversized on a lawn mower. Imagine how fast they are spinning on the highway. You could have four flat tires and not even know it till you slow down.

British cars are made with thin sheet metal and virtually no safety features except big windows that you can easily fly out of, hopefully landing in a quaint British haystack. So if you're driving one of the cars, you are out on the highway in a ball of aluminum foil. If you have an accident, your car will be scrunched up and thrown in the ditch like a chip bag. A British chip bag— oil and vinegar.

Different Countries, Different Cars

The fundamental problem with British cars in North America lies in the difference between the geography and culture of the nations. Britain is about the size of a mall. There's nowhere to go and all the time in the world to get there. Another factor is that the British are extremely class-conscious. It's only right and proper and traditional that the lower classes have crappy cars while the aristocracy gets peaches and cream. In North America, we are far more equal and democratic—here everyone gets crap.

The Bottom Line

The British are fine people and really funny to listen to, but their cars don't have a chance. This is not their finest hour. It's time for them to keep a stiff upper lip and announce to the world that they are finally giving up on their automotive industry—and are going to buy Japanese cars like the rest of us.

HOW TO SPEND QUALITY TIME WITH A CHILD

It's always a good thing for a father to spend time with his child in some activity or sport, or perhaps in a police chase. Many lifelong memories are created during those special times when Dad and the little one head out for a day at the Museum of Natural History and find themselves hopelessly lost in a discount mall. However, there are a few guidelines that can help you spend a day with your offspring without getting totally off-sprung.

First off, pick an activity that you really like to do. Despite their cute protests, all kids secretly love to go fishing. They just don't know it. They may insist they want to go to a theme park or a gang war of some kind, but they can do that on their own time, and besides, what do they know? Whatever you decide to do, get an early start—4:30 a.m. is a good target. That way, your son or daughter will want to come home before your relationship starts to deteriorate.

Okay, now it's important that this also be an educational experience for the child, so make sure there are lots of chances to learn as much as possible. Like how to carry stuff, and how to make a comfortable seat for both of you, and how to run and get things that you ask for throughout the duration of the fun. Children learn by doing. And fetching. And lifting.

After you've arrived and one of you has made twenty-seven trips back to the car to get something and you have everything set up and have assembled all your fishing gear and set your lines and made yourselves comfortable and there's nothing left to do but enjoy the day, PACK EVERYTHING UP AND GO HOME. This is very important. The only enjoyable part of the outing—i.e., the anticipation—is now over and you have entered the dangerous part of the adventure—i.e., the reality.

The reality never matches the anticipation. After all, what child ever anticipated arguing, fighting, insulting, getting cold, catching nothing, finding out the boat leaks, and sinking in ice cold water? If you don't have the courage to pack up and go home, you will see the following behaviour pattern develop, and it will be difficult for you to handle.

Phase One: The Twitch

Remember, children can't sit still. They start asking annoying questions about the sky. They keep fiddling with the fishing rod. They want to try a sip of whatever is in the flask you keep drinking from. They mention their favourite cartoon show, which they'd be watching if they were home right now. Then your child—the same one who can't remember to shut the screen door or pick up his or her clothes—will describe in intimate detail all 214 levels of some video game, including what you have to do to get past each level and the maximum number of points you can earn and the highest scores that he and every one of his friends have ever got.

Phase Two: The Placation

To hold the child's attention, you serve lunch. Even though it's 8 a.m. He doesn't like anything except the cookies, which he accidentally drops in the river. He turns his nose up at the huge baloney/ham/roast beef/peanut butter sandwiches you made. He opens a can of pop all over you and then falls on the sandwiches, knocking them down into the oil-filled bottom of the boat, giving them such a horrible taste that you can hardly keep them down. He starts crying, and other fishermen move away from the area. You envy the other fishermen. Finally your child settles down, quietly and peacefully, and then suddenly he vomits right into the minnow pail.

Phase Three: The Confrontation

The child starts to imply that the adventure is over. He has packed up all his stuff. He asks if he can sit in the car and read maps. You tell him that if he wants to go home, he should just say so. He just says so. You say, "Was that a wolf I saw on the shore?" He stares at the shore for about ten minutes before realizing you were lying. He starts whining about going home. You argue for a few minutes. You put your foot down and he pouts. After two minutes, the pouting is driving you nuts and scaring the fish away. You start to wish there *was* a wolf on the shore. You wind in your line, making a lot of noise and acting really disappointed. You get a nibble. You ignore it.

Phase Four: The Silence

On the drive home, your thoughts are not interrupted by any conversation or movement as the child sits quietly and stares out the window. About a block from your house, he puts a hand on your shoulder and thanks you for a great day and says, "Can't wait to tell Mom about everything we did." When you get in the door, the child regales your wife with stories of wolves, oil sandwiches, and throwing up in the bait pail. Your wife nods and smiles at the child, then quietly tells you she'll never understand the attraction of fishing.

Phase Five: The Revelation

You find yourself leafing through a Disney World brochure.

BUCKING TRENDS

I have a friend in the real estate business, and he was telling me how popular condos are with retirees. He then proceeded to list all the things that people no longer want in a home, which ended up being a pretty accurate description of the house I currently own.

Now, I know the logical decision would be for me to sell my house immediately at a huge loss and go and live in a condo with other people who have done the same thing, and then we could all get together on Saturday nights and reminisce about the good old days when we had backyards and garages. But I'm not going to do that.

There are two things I don't like about trends. First, trends are like breezes—they have to keep moving to exist. So once you start following trends, you're pretty much committing to a life on the road. Second, trends are for the sole purpose of making money. I'd rather eke out a living doing something I enjoy than make a fortune doing something I hate.

Maybe one day I'll be able to make a fortune doing something I enjoy. But that won't be a trend—it'll be a miracle.

WHEN NOT TO SAY WHAT YOU'RE THINKING

- While the policeman is writing out the ticket.
- When your minister asks if you know any good jokes.
- While you're at your in-laws' house, sitting at the dining room table staring at the contents of your dinner plate.
- When the boss asks how you like his haircut.
- When your wife says, "What's your problem?"

IN CASE OF AN ACCIDENT

(Cut this out and carry it in your car)

- Remove your seat belt. If you weren't wearing your seat belt, remove the shards of windshield.
- Check all your passengers and make sure everyone agrees on the same story to tell the cops.
- Check for injuries. If none, immediately decide who will fake what for the insurance.
- If there's any part of your car that is not damaged but you would like to have repaired free, damage it.
- Extinguish all smoking materials, including cigarettes, cigars, pipes, and passengers.
- Retrieve all passengers who were not wearing seat belts from nearby trees, ravines, rockslides, and under other vehicles.
- If there are flammable fluids spilled on the ground, mark out the perimeter of the spill with lit flares.
- If the other driver is behaving in an upset or aggressive manner, hit first and ask questions later. One bruise more won't matter.
- Make sure you have your licence, ownership, and bribe money for witnesses.

HOW TO TELL WHEN YOU NEED A VACATION

A lot of people are working too hard these days. Here are some danger signs to watch for:

- You always look like you've had seven coffees.

- You come home from work and your entire family has their bathing suits on.
- You only ride elevators that feature reggae music.
- You put a tiny umbrella into your glass of Maalox.
- You look for a tie that goes with your Hawaiian shirt.
- You have money in the bank.
- When you smile, your wife doesn't recognize you.

YOU'VE DONE A LOT BY COMPARISON

It's human nature to compare ourselves with others, but sometimes as we get older, we need to look outside our own circle—or even species—in order to feel that we haven't done badly. Take, for example, the sea turtle. It can live for a hundred years and yet its only accomplishment of any significance is laying eggs in the sand. You do that every month in the boardroom and you probably won't make it past seventy-five. Or look at those giant redwood sequoia trees, or whatever they're called. Some are more than two thousand years old, and they're famous because people drive through them. Well, you let people walk all over you and you're only forty-seven. So I say you're doing just fine. Maybe if you lived to be two hundred we could expect more, but let's not wish for too much of a good thing.

BODY CHECK

I was in a golf tournament recently and I couldn't help noticing that the young lady in the refreshment cart was significantly underdressed. I'm not complaining. I'm just saying I didn't know where to look. Well, actually I did know where to look—I just didn't think I could get away with it.

I understand that people dress that way to attract the attention of members of the opposite sex, especially in their own age group. But this was a golf tournament made up mostly of old guys like me, so I figure her outfit was mainly a marketing ploy. And it was working. She was doing a brisk business and her tip jar was just one more thing about her that was full to overflowing. There were no victims here, so I decided to feel good about it. I elected to treat it as a medical checkup. If I could look at a beautiful young woman and have an emotional response, that would mean my body is still working. And if I could do that without in any way thinking she might find me attractive, that would mean my brain must be okay too.

THE BALANCE OF NATURE

I'm a great believer in maintaining a balance in the types of friends you cultivate. If you're a middle-aged married guy, it's important to hang out with an old married guy and a young engaged guy. That way, you're ready to deal with every personal scenario. When you're feeling confused and troubled, you can talk to the old guy and find out that he's just as confused and troubled as you are, which means it obviously won't kill you. And when you're feeling successful and omnipotent, you can go and play squash with the young guy.

A GUIDE TO STREAMLINING

Nowadays, cars have really fancy streamlined bodies. Although anything you can afford will have a big, boxy, and ugly body. (I'll resist the temptation to point out the similarities to you personally.)

Of course, streamlining isn't new. We had streamlining back when I was a teenager. In fact, racing cars were really streamlined, with lightweight aluminum bodies that looked like this . . .

Unfortunately, your car doesn't look like that. It's not made of aluminum—it's made of rust. And it looks like this . . .

But now you too can have a streamlined, racy-looking car. All you need to do is take that fourteen-foot aluminum boat you accidentally drove over the rocks last summer . . .

Then remove all the metal body parts from your car. (Don't discard these, because I'm sure you'll think of some great project you can use them for, like a walk-in closet or a spare bedroom.)

Next, take the boat and remove the outboard motor, again saving it because you might be able to use it someday for something, or maybe the guy who owns the boat may figure out that you took it and want it back.

Now turn the boat over and mount it on the car frame like this:

Add paddles at the back for fins, and there you go. Your very own Puntiac. Or an Oldsmoboat.

Now I actually took this a bit further, because when I removed some of the body panels, the engine fell out. So I took the outboard motor and mounted it on the back like this:

Then I duct-taped it in place, removed the prop and turned it into a hood ornament, and attached paddles to the propeller shaft of the motor. This car is now my biggest fan.

I started her up and what do you know . . .

I got a hundred dollars for it from the scrap metal dealer.

HOW TO BE REGRETFUL

I know that people tend to have regrets in their lives, and as they get older, these regrets can become debilitating. But you can't go back and change any of them, and they can actually stop you from doing things now, out of fear that you'll regret those things later. They tell me you must have regrets to be normal, though, so to keep the real bad ones out of my mind, I've made a list of reasonable regrets that are bad enough to make me feel a slight twinge of guilt, but not so terrible that I end up hating myself. Here are my regrets:

- Buying a car made in a Baltic country.
- Eating that second pizza.
- Not going to the bathroom before riding the Scrambler.
- Not kissing my second girlfriend.
- Kissing my first girlfriend.
- Pulling Grandpa's finger.

NO PEAKING

A lot of guys I know have a photograph of themselves in great physical shape. Maybe they were on the rowing team or running every day, or maybe they just had the time and motivation to work out on a regular basis. So they have this picture of themselves with a small waist and rippling muscles. It might be on a guy's desk or somewhere in his home, or even worse, it's buried deep in his mind. Every time he sees or even thinks about that picture, he is reminded of how the aging process has destroyed him. It's been a constant deterioration from that earlier peak of physical prowess to the pitiful, flabby, lethargic, bald specimen he has now become.

I, on the other hand, have a picture of myself on the beach at the age of thirteen. My weight was within ten pounds of what it is now, and there is no physical evidence of any type of muscle. I can stand beside that picture at any time and comfort myself that I have not "started to sag" or "let myself go" or "lost a step." I was out of shape at thirteen, and I've maintained it all these years. Nobody looks at my picture and says, "Wow, is that you?"

Instead of looking good for a year or two and then feeling bad my whole life, I opted for looking bad all the time and feeling good my whole life.

ARE YOU UP FOR IT?

There is a peculiar disease that has plagued the men in my family. In fact, it seems to apply to almost all men in all families. I think it's called Riser's Syndrome. There's only one easy-to-spot symptom: as you get into middle age and beyond, you find yourself getting up earlier and earlier. A man who used to sleep till lunch at twenty-seven will leap out of bed at the crack of dawn at forty-eight.

And the disease seems to progress as you get older. Generally, you get up an hour earlier for every ten years of your age. If you were getting up at seven when you were thirty, you'll get up at six at forty, you'll get up at five at fifty, and so on. If you live long enough, you actually run the risk of getting up before you go to bed. That's why older men start back-timing their bedtime. We yawn through dinner, nap on the couch, and generally try to hit the sack by 9:30 p.m. This can be very inconvenient for our wives and family, not to mention our dinner guests.

So I've come up with a solution. If you're going to bed at 9 p.m. and getting up at 5 a.m., you're getting eight hours' sleep—they're just not the right eight hours. You need to move east—two time zones east, to be precise, where 9 p.m. becomes 11 p.m. and 5 a.m. becomes 7 a.m. That's acceptable for anybody. And in another ten years, you'll have to move farther east. Keep doing this and you will always be keeping proper hours, no matter how old you get. Besides, I hear China is a great place to live.

HOW TO USE YOUR CAR TO GET WOMEN

Nothing turns women on faster than a great car, and nothing turns them off faster than the guy who's driving it. The trick is to accessorize your car so that it screams "hunk," and then keep your mouth shut or the relationship will go "thunk."

The Colour

Women like flash. The kind of flash you do with a paint job, that is, rather than a raincoat. Paint your car a flashy colour: red, silver, deep blue. Avoid yellow, brown, and plaid. Be careful when choosing murals for your van. Horses and rock groups and spaceships are okay, but paintings of nude babes tend to attract gay women or, worse still, straight men.

Bumper Stickers

Decals are a reflection of your personality. "I Brake for Stray Dogs" suggests sensitivity, but "I Brake for Stray Dogs When I'm Hungry" sends a whole other message, and "I Brake for Stray Dogs When I'm Lonely" is just disturbing. You can send out the message that you're a worldly, well-travelled guy with bumper stickers that say "Talladega Speedway Is for Lovers," "We Saw the World's Largest Road Apple," or "I'd Rather Be in Go-Kart Universe, Wisconsin." People generally believe that all signs lie, so having a decal that reads "I'm a Swell Guy" or "I'm Way Cool" or "Tested Negative" sends the exact opposite message. Try one that says "I'm Willing to Give Women One Final Chance—Apply Within." It's just the kind of challenge that women can't resist.

Fur

If you really want to impress the ladies, you've got to get fun-fur seat covers in Day-Glo pink or tiger stripes. Trust me. And don't just use old shag carpeting from your deck or try stretching out a velour sweater you got at a Star Trek convention. Spend the money and get the proper seat covers. They cost a bit, but they'll save you a lot in flowers and candy.

Wheel Disks

It's been my experience that most women don't know the difference between, say, a 'Cuda and a HemiCuda. It's true. But they do recognize a great set of wheel disks. If you're going out at nights, you can probably get away with a set of garbage can lids sprayed silver.

Add-ons

Mud flaps on the rear tires and a big leather cover to prevent the hood from stone chips also send a message that you are a sensitive, caring guy. At least when it comes to your car. And a woman is naturally curious to find out if you will have the same respect and concern for her. Even though no other guy she's met with a car like yours did. The design on the mud flaps can make or break your chances. A top hat or a die looks very classy. A silhouette of a naked woman can be scary. Especially if you traced it.

Lights

The more lights you have adorning your vehicle the better. Cover the grill, the side mirrors, the rear window, and all the window trim with lights, then add fluorescent ground effects and even a laser beam coming out of your tailpipe. The appearance that the sun shines out of your exhaust pipe gets respect. If you have enough disposable income to completely cover your car with lights, do it. (Right after Christmas, hardware stores sell off strings of lights dirt cheap.) If you have enough bulbs, you can make your car look like something out of *Close Encounters of the Third Kind*, or that electric light parade at Disney World, or maybe even a galaxy. Stars give off light. If you give off light, you must be a star. (Don't assume that hanging a moon will enhance this image.)

Sound

LOUD! Jack up the car and look along the exhaust pipe until you see a section that's bigger than the rest. That's the muffler. Hack the muffler off with a pickaxe. Now you've got some serious engine noise happening. Next, find a punk rock band that's bankrupt. That shouldn't be hard. If all you find is a punk rock band that's doing well, wait a week. Buy all their equipment cheap or trade them for razor blades. Pile all the speakers and amps into your back seat and hook them up to your radio. Turn the bass up to where the car is hopping off the pavement and doing the Macarena. This not only lets the women know you can dance, but also tells the Catholic girls that you understand rhythm. (Do not turn the radio to an all-talk station. Women don't like guys who are all talk.)

Make and Model

Don't waste your money here. Only other guys care that it's a 1968 Boss Chevy Nova in mint with Harley carbs, and you don't want to attract guys, remember? Women couldn't care less what kind of car it is. Once women see the lights and hear the racket, they'll have made up their minds.

The Last Word

The key is to find a way not to be ignored. If you deck your car out the way I've described, the women will definitely notice. If they're pointing and laughing, you can sneak around on foot and join them with comments like "Look at that piece of crap. What a loser." Have a few laughs with them about it. They'll like you. You'll probably get to take them home. Call a cab. If you're lucky, you won't have to come and get your car till the morning.

HOW TO TELL WHEN YOUR COMPANY IS ABOUT TO DOWNSIZE

- During the lunch break, nobody can find the want ads because your boss has them.
- Your company just had a bad year. Or a good year. Or an average year.
- The company president traded in his BMW for a Hyundai.
- Extra boxes of Kleenex are brought in for the directors' meeting.
- The company replaces the nurse with someone named Kevorkian.
- Your office is being used to store Star Wars merchandise.
- Your boss tells the courier about your excellent work habits and asks if his company is hiring.
- Your request for a pay increase is met with stunned silence, then laughter.
- Everyone in senior management is spending most of the day in the restroom.
- You have shareholders.

YOU'RE NOT GETTING OLDER, YOU'RE GETTING MORE FOCUSED

Some people see the aging process as the law of diminishing returns. I prefer to look at it as nature's way of coordinating knowledge, experience, and focus. As you lose your hair and vision and hearing and libido and general degree of attractiveness to members of the opposite sex—or any sex, of any species—you're left to concentrate on your true purpose in life. I'm still not completely sure what that is, but for me it's trending toward some combination of eating junk food, watching television, and complaining. I'm sure I'll have a clearer picture any day now. I'll keep you posted.

HOW TO BUY TIRES

Tires are expensive. Why they can't make a tire that will carry a ton of metal at one hundred miles an hour for at least fifty thousand miles for less than ten dollars is beyond me. That's just the kind of corporate gouging John and Jane Consumer have to live with. So here are a few tire suggestions that can save you big bucks.

No-Name Tires

No-name tires can be bought at discount prices. Make sure you examine them carefully, though. They could be seconds, and in a race against time, you want more than seconds. On the other hand, they could be perfectly good tires that just didn't sell for some reason. Maybe the whitewalls are more of an off-white, or maybe the word "ply" is misspelled or the tread mark says "I'm a dork." Chances are these tires were made in the same way and the same factory as the expensive tires. They are every bit as good. Look for "Made in USA" or "Made in Japan." Avoid "Made in Madagascar."

And be careful that they are not in fact homemade tires from somebody's basement rubber-manufacturing kit. Is the brand just a guy's name, like Bob or Herbie? Are there tools sticking out of the sidewalls? Are the treads in the same pattern as a pie crust? Is the tire made from a bunch of erasers glued together? When you come over the crest of a hill at eighty miles an hour to find a flock of sheep on the road, you'll be sorry you went with the Herbie Stove-bolted Roadial.

Used Tires

Used tires are your cheapest source of quality rubber. If you're not concerned about all four tires being exactly the same colour or shape or size—or for the same vehicle—you can pick up hundreds of freebies just by going to a mall after dark with a pile of trunk keys. Most people never use their spare, and if they're at the mall, that proves they're shoppers, so they'll probably thank you for the extra trunk space. Just stay clear of the little space-saver spares. They can make a Lincoln Town Car look like a hippo in high heels.

Making Your Tires Last Longer

When a car is standing still, 90 percent of the tire is not even touching the ground. There is no more effective way of making your tires last than not moving your car. If for any reason you do have to move the car, don't forget the laws of physics. Particularly the tangential and centrifugal forces exerted on a rotating object. What this means is that the faster your tire is spinning, the rounder it becomes. And the rounder it becomes, the less contact it has with the road. The less contact with the road, the longer the tire will last. The ultimate would be for the tire to have no contact with the road whatsoever. (Yes, it's true that many accidents have occurred when a vehicle loses contact with the road, but on the upside, the tires are often in very good condition for resale.)

At rest, a tire is almost flat on one side. At eight hundred miles an hour, it is believed to be perfectly round (although nobody's ever had the guts to lean out and look). So if your car can't be at rest, you should try to get as close to eight hundred miles an hour as possible. (Drivers who commute down Mt. Fuji rarely complain of tire wear.)

Don't use a garage in winter. A frozen tire lasts longer. Plus there's a better chance your car won't start, and that's the ultimate tread saver (see above).

Alter your driving patterns to suit your tires. Brand-new tires in peak condition are designed to handle the roughest road conditions, from huge potholes to fresh, sharp gravel. As the tire tread wears, all you need to do is change where you're driving. Switch to the absolute smoothest of roads to make it easier on the tire. When even that's getting dicey, move to the sidewalks, which are smooth cement. And when your tires are on their last legs, drive into town on your neighbours' lawns.

Make your tire puncture-proof by letting out the air and removing the bleeder valve, and then take your caulking gun and inject about forty-three tubes of bathtub sealer into the tire. Now when the tread wears out, you'll still have lots of rubber to go.

Even when your tires are finished, you can still use them to make lawn ornaments or driveway liners or soup bowls or earrings. Cover your home with tire art as a statement to the world: "I may be bald with bulges in the side and a lot of miles on me, but I can still give you a belt, so tread lightly." Or it might just say, "I need stronger medication."

GOING TO THE DOGS

They say that as people get older, they really start to appreciate a pet. Some of the retirement homes bring in dogs regularly as therapy for the residents. Once you have a few miles on you, you're apparently ready to lower your standard of social interaction to the canine level. Personally I don't understand the appeal of spending so much time and energy on something that can't talk to you. Or talk back to you. Or borrow your car without asking. Or use your money to flunk out of college. Or ruin its life and then blame you. But then, maybe that's just me.

LOWER THE BAR AND PULL UP A STOOL

When I was in high school, my friends and I were exposed to a lot of hype from the guidance department on striving for excellence and being the best and always making sure that our reach exceeded our grasp. Frankly, that's created a lot of problems for all of us. Now that we're a little older, we've given up on excellence and being the best, and many of us are down to our last grasp. The end result of forty-odd years of striving for unattainable goals is a deep sense of failure and worthlessness. This is not good. We need to reverse this trend by finding success in our lives. It's time to lower the bar. Here is a list of accomplishments that you can look at and say, "Hey, I'm a star!":

- You have some kind of a job and live in some kind of dwelling.
- You have never spent more than a night or two in jail.
- At some point in your life, you've been able to get a loan.
- You've never killed anyone on purpose.
- You're not a quitter. You didn't quit those jobs—you were fired.
- You have never had an extramarital affair with a supermodel.
- When you go into a clothing store, you can still find one or two items that are too big for you.

- Although you've never been on A&E's <u>Biography</u>, you've also never been on <u>America's Most Wanted</u>.
- You have never done nearly as many stupid things as you've thought of.
- You don't whine.

SURVEILLANCE TO LOOK OUT FOR

Now that we have satellites and miniature cameras and the crime rate seems to be under control, I'd like to see the whole surveillance industry become more service-oriented. Here are a few spy applications that I'd like to see:

- Let me see how unhappy all the girls who dumped me in high school are now.
- Let me hear what people say about me immediately after I leave the room.
- Let me see a room in my company where nobody ever goes. Is it big enough for a cot?
- Let me see my boss talking about me with his wife.
- Let me see my boss talking about anything with somebody else's wife.
- Let me see what's waiting for me when I come home late.
- Let me see what's waiting for me when I come home early.

DON'T GET TOO COMFORTABLE

Every generation gets a little wimpier than the one before it. Our ancestors lived in wooden shacks without running water or electricity. We have central heating, central air, central vac, central casting, humidifiers, dehumidifiers, carbon filters, ozone detectors, smoke detectors, chest protectors, bomb deflectors, and house inspectors. We can push one button in our house and another in our car, and as long as we have an attached garage, we will never leave an atmosphere of constant temperature, humidity, oxygen content, and clarity. It makes for an easy, comfortable life, but over time Mother Nature will devolve us to the point where we can't handle any change in our environment. Sure, it might be nice never to shiver or sweat but not if it means that every time you open the fridge or oven door, you have a massive cardiac infarction.

So don't try so hard to make it so easy. Human beings survive a lot better when they have something to fight against. That's why married people live longer.

DRESSING FOR TROUBLE

I sometimes take abuse for my wardrobe. I tend to be on the low side of casual. A flannel shirt and tattered jeans are my uniform of choice. It's not an unconscious selection. I'm very aware of why I dress like that. First of all, I think it sends out a good message that I'm not using my clothes to make you think I'm rich or important. I'm important to me, and while I'm happy to have you join me in that opinion, it's your call. My clothes also send a message to single women that I'm out of bounds. If I dress this shabby while I'm looking, can you imagine how bad it will be after she gets to know me? (My wife has never totally bought this argument.)

But the main reason I dress this way is because I think you have to be ready for anything: a leaky pipe, a lawn mower that won't start, or a car that needs a push. When there's an emergency, I can just jump right in. I don't need to find a phone booth to change in. So when you see a guy decked out in extra-casual wear, you know he's dressed for battle. And when you see a guy in an expensive suit, you know that if you have an emergency, he'll be grabbing his cellphone and calling somebody like me.

HOW TO AVOID BUYING THE WRONG USED CAR

There's nothing more frustrating than buying what you think is a good-quality used car, only to have it disintegrate into components or explode in a massive fireball. You need to know what to look for when you're examining a car. An ounce of prevention is worth a ton of tow truck.

Here are some bad signs:

- The car is fourteen years old and has less than two thousand miles on it. Check for claw-hammer marks around the odometer.
- The tires are grey wood.
- The trunk is full of parts. Not spare parts. Just parts.
- The engine is covered in duct tape. Either the block is cracked or the owner is.
- The interior is heavily charred.
- The door handles are the same ones you have on your kitchen cupboards.
- When you start the engine, you can't see, hear, smell, or taste for a full five minutes.
- The lucky dice hanging from the rear-view mirror have been shredded by incoming bullets.
- On closer inspection, you notice that the tires are just inner tubes with a tread drawn on in Magic Marker.

- Everything below the windows is soaking wet, and there are fish in the glove compartment.
- The ownership papers are written in crayon and sealed with a potato stamp.
- The front end is smashed in and the brake pedal is bent in half.
- When you put on the emergency brake, the owner fakes the clicking sounds.
- The words "Police road block" are imprinted backwards in the grill.
- The car has been banned from the AAA.
- Magnets don't stick to the car's body. They do stick to the owner's head.
- It's one year old and has more than two hundred thousand miles on it.
- It's a convertible, but it wasn't when it was built.
- The owner won't let you stand closer than fifty feet to inspect it, and he insists you squint when you look at it.
- The back seat looks like it was used in <u>Pulp Fiction</u>.
- The body looks like it was used in <u>Ben-Hur</u>.
- If you want the body with the engine, that's extra.
- The paint is still wet.
- The owner answers every inquiry with "I refuse to answer that on the grounds it might incriminate me."

And the best reason not to buy:

- The car belongs to somebody you know.

HOW TO DO YOUR OWN CAR MAINTENANCE

You can save yourself a lot of time and money by working on your own car. Cars have got much simpler through the years. You don't have to set the spark timing or hand crank the engine anymore. It's amazing how a little common sense can save you so much money and give you the satisfaction of knowing that whatever goes wrong, you were involved.

Checking the Fluids

Like your kids before every trip, the fluids in your car must be checked on a regular basis. The rad, the windshield washers, the power steering, the master cylinder, the engine, the transmission, and the differential are all things designed to have liquids in them. Much like your uncle.

And speaking of dipsticks, they are there to help you check the levels. Pull the oil dipstick out of your engine and wipe it off on your shirt. If it's a good shirt, wipe it in the armpit. Reinsert the dipstick and remove it again. If you see any fluid at all on the dipstick, that's good enough. Yes, they have a mark for "Full," which is supposedly the amount of oil you're supposed to have. But don't forget that mark was put there by the oil companies. It's more of a marketing ploy than an automotive rule. Besides, if you're low on oil, the engine is obviously burning it or leaking it, so why throw good money after bad?

Some fluids don't have a dipstick. The rad and steering box and windshield washer should just be filled till they overflow. They each use different liquids, but if you're stuck, light beer works well in any environment. Ask your kidneys.

The differential is the toughest. Remove the filler plug. If nothing drips out, you can assume that it's almost full and is probably fine. If you're driving along and it seizes up, which locks your rear wheels and forces the car into a series of doughnuts and figure eights on the highway, add more fluid.

Checking Tire Pressure

If you don't have a proper tire gauge, use a pea shooter. Slip the pea shooter over the valve, drop in a pea, then tilt the valve to release the pressure. (Do not look down the end of the shooter to see if the pea is coming.) A tire at normal pressure in zero wind conditions can fire a pea more than two hundred yards or lodge it three inches into a human buttock. (Don't ask.) If the pea doesn't go that far, or in fact drops into the tire, you need air. Inflate the tire until just before it explodes.

Checking Lights

The hard part of checking your lights, after you get past the apathy, is checking the brake lights when you're alone. (If you're reading this book, you're probably alone a lot.) It's not physically possible to step on the brake pedal and run fast enough to get around the back to see if the lights went on. There's a simple solution, though. Pull onto the highway and look for a truck with a big, shiny grill. As soon as you pass the truck, cut in front of him and slam on your brakes. You should be able to see the reflection of your brake lights in his grill. (If he hits you, you'll have to recheck them.)

THE RIGHT CONNECTIONS

Like most people my age, I've been dragged kicking and screaming into the Information Age, the world of the Internet and email and the reclassification of the disadvantaged to include people with only one phone line. I don't know what software you're using, but the stuff I'm on gives my connection rate whenever I go online. It says, "You're connected at 44,000 bps," or "You're connected at 37,000 bps," or whatever. This affects the speed at which I can download information. So I'm thinking this would be a handy thing to flash on an unseen screen in the back of my mind when I meet a new person at a party. If it says, "You are connected at 3 bps," I would know to speak slowly to this person, keep it simple, and move on as quickly as possible. If, on the other hand, it says, "You are connected at 3,000,000 bps," I'd know to pay attention and keep it interesting and move the conversation on as quickly as possible. I would also consider this person a potential life partner. Except for the fact that I'm already married. And when it comes to the connection speed with my wife, we're on cable.

PAY NOW, PAY LATER

I've been a consumer for a pretty long time, and except for a brief hiatus in the early nineties, I've done my part. I've bought my share of cars and boats and homes and appliances and tools. I've had situations where I felt I paid too much and others where I thought I got a real deal, but over time, I've come to the conclusion that everything costs the same. Either you can pay top dollar for a high-quality used car and have years of trouble-free driving, or you can buy some cheap beater and spend a fortune on repairs and tow trucks. Same with boats. Same with everything. My advice is to decide on the exact make and model you want and then shop for the best price, rather than buying the cheapest make and model you can find and then having to talk yourself into liking it. I'm very fond of this theory and truly wish I could afford it.

FIVE QUESTIONS THAT SCARE MARRIED MEN

1) Did you do what you promised to do?
2) Where did the apple pie go?
3) Do you remember what today is?
4) What size pants are you wearing these days?
5) Have you got big plans for later?

THE WHOLE WORLD IN YOUR HANDS

I find that generally women like to keep souvenirs and pictures and mementos a lot more than men do. We probably have half a dozen photo albums and boxes of kids' paintings in our house. Most men don't need that stuff. They can take a trip down memory lane just by looking at their own hands.

Take a few minutes on a Saturday morning and look at your hands. Turn them over slowly so you can see all the scars and nicks, and it's amazing how the memories will come flooding back. How can you look at that thumbnail without remembering the dock you built and then rebuilt, before hiring a guy who charged too much because he'd seen your work? When you notice the knuckle with the missing hair, it reminds you which hand you use to light the barbecue. Some of the marks bring back simple images: a chainsaw, a Cuisinart, a nail gun. Some of them remind you of locations: up on the roof looking down, followed immediately by down on the ground looking up; under the car; inside the furnace; over the steam valve; inside the ambulance.

But you don't want to look back too much. So drop your hands, pick up your tool box, take a couple of aspirins, and go and make some new memories.

HOW TO CONVERSE WITH YOUR WIFE

Here are five survival tips on how to keep a marriage smoking long after the fire has gone out:

1) Be very quiet when she's talking. If she stops talking, always wait a full minute before speaking. She may not be finished.

2) Do not change the subject. Even if you have to speak first, you can usually figure out what she wants to talk about. For example, if she's trying to clean an oil stain on the kitchen floor, she probably wants to talk about you trying to fix the lawn mower in the sink.

3) Watch her body language. Alter what you're saying in response to what she does. If she stops doing her nails and starts sharpening a knife, it's time for you to do a one-eighty.

4) Maintain eye contact. If you can't see her eyes, you have no idea how things are going. If you're working on the car and she asks you about plans for the weekend, take the time to roll out on the creeper so you can see her response, rather than just yelling, from under the car, "I'm going fishing with Bob—I told you that last week." Remember that she has access to heavy tools and the lower half of your body is exposed. Always maintain eye contact. Don't have conversations in the dark, and don't talk to your wife on the telephone unless you're a professional.

5) Keep your sentences short—five words maximum. That allows you to change quickly. If it's not going well, try saying "Unless" or "But" or "Whatever." Short sentences give her a chance to talk. Which is what you want. You want the conversation to go her way. It's not about success. It's about survival.

DANCES WITH DISASTER

There are a lot of things a man can do to fool everybody about his true age. For one thing, there are products out there to help: hair dyes and wrinkle cream; cosmetic surgery and toupees; contact lenses, laxatives, and Viagra. You can talk about things that younger people talk about. You can wear young clothes and drive a young person's car. You can even pretend to like young people's music. But it's all over when you hit the dance floor.

Once you start flailing away doing the Frug or the Monkey or the Loco-Motion, you've blown your cover. When people see you dance, they know you grew up with Chubby Checker. Even slow dances give you away, as you sway with your arm stuck straight out like a railway crossing. The horrible truth is that you have to make a choice: you must either be honest about your age or never, ever dance again. It's a tough one. My advice is to do both.

HOW TO SAY GOODBYE TO YOUR FAVOURITE CAR

No matter how much we do, there comes a time in the life of any car when we have to say goodbye. This can be upsetting and even traumatic for the owner, particularly if he still has two more years of car payments. Here are a few procedural steps you can take to ensure closure at this time of great emotional stress:

- Remove from the car everything that has any personal significance for you—the paper cups, the cigarette butts, the spent shells, your underwear, your passenger's underwear, the previous owner's underwear, the fuzzy dice, the dingle balls, the sex lights, the eight-tracks, the Garfield window sticker, the pizza boxes, the pizza.

99

- Leave anything that you never used—maps, napkins, air freshener, emergency brake, turn signals, owner's manual, rear-view mirror, seat belts.
- Step back from the car and think about the significant memories it holds for you—car chicken, car chase, car ceration; drag race, <u>Dragnet</u>, drag queen; prom night, promise night, prompt night; flat tire in the rain, small errors, medium impacts, big explosions.
- Say a silent prayer of thanks: "Dear Lord, thank you for making this car, and for making it run, and for making the previous owner leave the keys in it outside the 7-Eleven. Thank you for not allowing me to harm myself or other people with this car. Sorry about the raccoon. Amen."
- Turn and walk away—no second thoughts, no looking back. Forget the car. Go to the nearest ATM, take out fifty dollars, and buy another one just like it.

PSYCHOLOGIST, HEAL THYSELF

I have a couple of concerns about the whole self-help movement. The idea is that each of us is great and fantastic, and there's nothing we can't do if we just liberate ourselves from negative thoughts. I'm middle-aged, twenty pounds overweight, barely average height, with poor eye–hand coordination and a history of avoiding physical exertion. No amount of self-help will allow me to be the starting centre for the Chicago Bulls. And that's not just a negative thought—it's also a positive reality. The point is we *need* to have negative thoughts about ourselves. Negative thoughts keep us employed and married and allow us to get along with our friends and neighbours. Nothing kills a relationship faster than saying to yourself, "I could do better." Especially when the truth is that *they* could do better. Try to think of your ego as a hot air balloon. The positive thoughts keep it up, while the negative thoughts keep it down. The perfect altitude for you is just above the high-tension wires and just below the radar. Too many positive thoughts and you have too far to fall. Too many negative thoughts and you're dragging your basket.

THAT'S YOUR LIMIT

If any of you have worked in a high-pressure sales organization, then you're familiar with the concept of having a quota of sales or contacts that you're expected to meet. I'm beginning to think that the quota system is a natural phenomenon that occurs in all aspects of human behaviour.

Yesterday, I was trying to pull out of a side street. There were two cars approaching—the first was an elderly gentleman with his turn signal going, and the second was a teenager with no signal on. The first car didn't turn but the second one did. What that shows me is that when we're young, we don't use our turn signals, and then when we get old, we have to use them all the time because we need to meet our quota and we're running out of time.

And it's true with lots of activities. People who sit quietly now probably did way too much talking in the past. And it's usually the same with non-smokers and non-drinkers. They used up their quota. Maybe impotence is the ultimate acknowledgment of a job well done.

DON'T SWEAT THE BIG STUFF

I was watching an episode of *60 Minutes* last week and they had new evidence that life will eventually kill us. That show has been on the air for about a thousand years, and I wonder how they've managed to come up with new things for us to worry about every week. I bet if they went back over their old shows, they'd find all kinds of catastrophes that just never happened: banking machines are dangerous, or ozone depletion will bring the end of life as we know it in the next four years, or disco music causes spinal damage. I notice that the worries are getting larger these days. Instead of uncovering corruption in Nicaragua, they're now telling us that our air is poisoned, our water supply is polluted, the polar caps are melting, and we have more garbage dumps than farms.

I hate to sound irresponsible, but I've lost the ability to get upset about these horrible problems. I just need somebody to tell me what to do and I'll gladly do it. I'll boil my water or stop dancing or store my garbage in rubber. Whatever it takes. Just don't tell me I should be worrying about things I can't understand or control. No wonder *Seinfeld* was a hit.

HOW TO MAINTAIN YOUR PRIVACY

If you're fed up with neighbours and strangers coming to your front door to visit or to ask for your participation or to try to sell you something, here are some things to do that will keep them away:

- Place a "Watch for Land Mines" sign on your front lawn beside an exploded car.
- Keep a big dog on your porch, chewing a pant leg.

- Rewire your doorbell so that it plays a tape of gunshots.
- Cover your welcome mat with shards of broken beer bottles.
- Put one of those yellow police barrier tapes across the end of your driveway.
- On your front door hang a sign saying "Caution—Exorcism in Progress."
- Leave a pizza delivery car in your driveway with the door open and the engine running for a week or so.
- When you see someone approaching, start a chainsaw running inside the house.
- Place quarantine signs around your property.
- In the middle of the night, turn over a rectangle of your front lawn so that it looks like a fresh grave. Add another one every few months.

LET SLEEPING DOGS BE AN EXAMPLE TO YOU

We have a thirteen-year-old dog who doesn't look or listen as well as he used to, but apart from that, he seems just fine. They tell me he's ninety-one in human years, and I'd say he's got another thirty or so to go. I've been studying him to discover his secrets to longevity, hoping I could apply them to my own life. I ruled out drinking from the toilet bowl, and my wife kiboshed relieving myself on the lawn. That left the naps. My dog has about seven naps a day. That's a dog day. That equates to seven human days. In other words, to a dog, the time between naps is a day. What a great concept. That's something I should do. If I have four naps a day and count the space in between each as a day, it will completely change my life. Sure, it'll screw up my calendar, but I'll be well rested and I'll live to be 160.

TECHNO BABYLON

There is a misconception out there that technology makes us more efficient or saves us time. I don't agree. Yes, a microwave oven can reheat a slice of pizza faster and more efficiently than a normal oven, but first I have to go out and earn enough money to buy the microwave, so you have to add that time in. Then I have to read the instructions and set the clock. Then I have to pay for the electricity to run it. I know what you're going to say. "It's not as much electricity as a stove uses." Don't worry about it. I'll eat the pizza cold. That's faster than any microwave, and it doesn't cost a cent. So be careful when you're choosing technology. If it's something you really need in your life, great. But a lot of technology just gives us faster ways of doing unnecessary jobs.

BE GOOD AT WHAT YOU ENJOY BEING GOOD AT

My wife was talking about a friend of ours, commenting on how successful he'd been. We've been married long enough for me not to take that as a criticism, no matter how it was intended. I did say, though, that this guy really enjoys his job, and my wife answered, "That's why he's good at it."

I've heard that before, and I still don't agree with it. It's based on a fallacy. You're not good at something just because you enjoy it. Karaoke has proven that. To my way of thinking, you're not good at something because you enjoy it, but rather, you enjoy something because you're good at it. And you need to have proof that you're good at it. People have complimented you or you've won awards or been promoted. If you continue to do things without getting that kind of feedback, then your enjoyment is at the expense of someone else's suffering. You're not good at it. You're just at it. And the reason you enjoy it is because you're oblivious to the fact that others are allowing you to keep doing it because of stringent societal regulations concerning assault and homicide.

So in the future, please make sure you're good at something before you start to enjoy it. If we all do that, there'll be an instant upgrade in party jokes, after-dinner speeches, and honeymoons.

MY SECOND CUP RUNNETH OVER

One of the signs that our society is changing is the decline in the number of taverns in the community and the proliferation of coffee bars. We have them in malls, at airports, even in bookstores. Is this really a good idea? We have a population that's overworked and overstressed. Is more caffeine a good thing? I wonder how much of the end of civility in our society is directly attributable to that fourth cup of java. Road rage, arguments over a parking spot, jockeying for position when lining up—none of these situations is improved by the presence of Juan Valdez. When I see a guy on the news climbing a bell tower with an assault rifle, I wonder if things might have been different if he'd switched to decaf.

THE LIVING WILL

Breakthroughs in medical science are wreaking havoc on the tradition of each generation benefiting from the toils of the former one. In the old days, when mid-forties was the life expectancy, a man would pass away and leave his estate or his farm or his blacksmith tools or whatever to his son, who would be in his early twenties and could really use that stuff. Now we've got people living for eighty years and more, and it'll only get worse.

I think we'll see the time when it will be common for people to live past the age of one hundred. That'll really mess things up. What is the point of dying at the age of 110 and leaving everything to your ninety-year-old son? It's a little late. So you might think about leaving it to your grandson, who's only seventy. Or your great-grandson, who's fifty.

To really make a difference in someone's life, an inheritance has to come much earlier. So you'd end up leaving everything to your great-great-great-grandchildren, who are virtual strangers and barely blood relatives. Instead, I say your best bet is to spend the money before you die and spend it on somebody you know really well—yourself.

If my wife is reading this, that boat I've been looking at is still for sale.

CASH AND CARRY

There are many differences between men and women, and all of them are at least interesting. Many are even mind-boggling. For example, women have no respect for pockets, but men live for them. Pockets are a place to keep money, treasures, notes, car keys, your wallet, and your hands as a signal that you approach life as an uninvolved spectator. Women don't like pockets because they add bulk. Women are uncomfortable with bulk. The pocket itself adds two layers of material, and if you put something in it, it's even worse. Women prefer to use a purse. And it's not just the bulk thing. Women carry more equipment—makeup and hair devices and various personal items. No garment would ever have enough pockets. So as odd as it may seem, I say we just leave well enough alone. Let the women stay with the purses. If they ever switch to pockets and then start standing around with their hands in them, that would only mean more work for us men.

GET IT IN WRITING

Engineers keep coming up with new gadgets and then salesmen have to figure out why we consumers need them. It's a phenomenon called "technology in search of a market." Well, I think I can help. I saw this gadget recently. It's like a little computerized Dictaphone that you talk into and it converts what you say into text that you can read. The words come up on a little screen, and you can print them off or save them on your computer or just look at them and marvel at your own genius. Well, I have a great application for this product. Instead of using it on yourself, use it to record what other people say. Everybody's pretty fast and loose with oral communication, but there's still a healthy respect for the written word. Just think if you'd recorded your wife's voice that one time in your twenty-year marriage when you both knew you were right. Or that time your boss got into the eggnog and promised you a job for life. Wouldn't it be a great way to immortalize what you've been told? Expressions like "Your car will be ready by three o'clock," or "Your home will never go down in value," or "Don't worry, I'm sure it's just a mole" would be captured for all eternity.

EARLY PAROLE FOR LOW-HANDICAP GOLFERS

There's been a lot of discussion about early parole for serious offenders, and the big question is always whether they are fully rehabilitated. I have a suggestion: allow these prisoners to play golf for at least six months prior to their parole application. If they can get their handicap down to under fifteen, then they should be set free. If not, they have no control over their bodies and parole should be denied. If this rule were ever applied to me, I would spend my entire life behind bars, which in some ways would be kinder than allowing me to continue playing golf.

THINGS THAT GO FAST

Everything seems to be going faster and faster these days—cars and rockets and people's lives. I think Einstein proved that everything is relative or something like that, and it's never truer than it is with speed. Now that I've lived a bit, I have a better perspective on what rate of motion is. Here's a list of things that really do go fast:

- Your knees
- Your cash
- Spicy food
- Time spent in the proctologist's waiting room
- The time between your birthdays
- Your engagement
- Your honeymoon
- Your new car warranty
- Your moments of brilliance
- Your hairline
- Your waistline
- Your timeline

GREY HORSEPOWER

I was driving into the city yesterday and I was speeding. I was at least 20 percent over the speed limit when I went right by a parked police car, but the officer didn't chase me or signal me to pull me over. That's because I was pretty much the slowest car on the road. Everybody speeds now. The average car today goes much faster than the average car of thirty years ago. Yet the average driver today is much older than the average driver of thirty years ago. Does that make sense to you? Is it a good idea that as our population ages, we give them more horsepower? Think about your own grandfather—his eyesight, his hearing, his reaction time, his alertness, his sleepy leg. Please don't allow him to be at the wheel of a speeding car. You must put the safety of others ahead of your impatience for the inheritance.

HOW TO INSTALL AN AQUARIUM SKYLIGHT

Here's a quick, easy way to install your own skylight in your truck or van. A skylight will beautify your van, increase its value, and make it more fun to drive. It's such a sure-fire hit, in fact, you'll be tempted to do it to your own vehicle. But I suggest you work out the bugs first by trying it on a friend's.

Okay, let's create the opening for the skylight first. Get up on the roof and eyeball where you want the skylight to go. Over the driver's seat is a good spot. You'll be cutting a rectangle with a reciprocating saw, but first grab a pickaxe and make a decent-sized pilot hole.

Cut the hole out with the saw. (Make sure it's a rental saw, or better still, borrow one from a friend.) Now lay some caulking around the edge to make 'er waterproof. You don't want rain dripping down the back of your neck. In fact, you might want to put caulking around the collar of your shirt just to be on the safe side. Now you're ready for the glass.

You know, the difference between a handyman and a hobbyist is the ability to take somebody else's hobby and turn it into something handy. The handy thing is a van skylight. The hobby thing is an aquarium. Find an empty aquarium (or empty a found aquarium) and use that as your skylight. It's light and strong and waterproof. All you have to do is put it on the roof upside down. Sure, it might smell a little fishy, but then so does the van. And it'll be real handy if you're ever lost and need to look around, because you can pop your head right up into the aquarium, like a turret.

If you really want to push the envelope, mount the aquarium skylight on the side of your van, near the back, for that kid who's always asking, "Are we there yet? Are we there yet?" Now he can stick his head into the aquarium and see for himself.

BEFORE BEST BEFORE

When I was growing up, we didn't have "best before" stickers on anything. If the milk smelled okay, you drank it. If the meat was somewhere in the vicinity of its original colour, you ate it. If the can had rust only on the outside, you ate the contents. That doesn't happen anymore. Now everyone demands the best. That's why people are up on the night of January 11 finishing off the "best before Jan 12" ice cream. And they wonder why we're all overweight. I wonder if this "best before" concept will expand to include friends and family. Can you picture Uncle Ernie with a sticker saying "Best before second martini"? Or Grandpa's saying "Best before 7 p.m."? Or your own saying, "Best before 1971"?

THE TRUTH AS WE KNOW IT

Has this ever happened to you? You're out with your spouse at a social function, and she starts pontificating on a topic about which she knows nothing. Coincidentally, it's a topic about which you know a great deal—your business or your investment or you personally. And what's worse, she's making all kinds of false statements and exaggerations. If you've been married only a short time, there's a temptation to correct your spouse in front of others. You will soon learn that the truth not only does hurt but it is usually a self-inflicted wound. So don't ever correct your partner in a group. Nor should you stand behind her and make hand gestures indicating to the others that you think your spouse is a little wacko. No, your job is to move away slowly or pretend you're not listening or act drunk. The truth is for church or the courts. When the truth comes out at parties, it's only going to make trouble.

HOW TO TELL WHEN YOU'RE BEING DOMINATED

We all know that the best relationships are close to a fifty-fifty partnership. Here are the signs that perhaps one partner is dominating the other:

- There is an old rusty car abandoned in the front yard.
- The husband and wife wear matching shirts.
- The family dog is a cat.
- The family vehicle is a motorcycle with a sidecar.
- The beer fridge is the one in the kitchen.
- One of them wears an "I'm with stupid" T-shirt.
- One of them keeps the TV remote on their person.
- The welcome mat says "Trespassers will be shot."
- The lawn is covered with cutouts of fat people bending over.
- There's a couch on the front porch. There's also a guy sleeping on it.

KEEP YOUR SHIRT ON

I like to watch football on TV, but I find that lately it's getting violent and offensive and the camera coverage is far too graphic. Of course I'm talking about those shots of inebriated fans with their shirts off. There was a guy on last night's game sporting a bad green-and-gold paint job on a gut so massive he must have used a roller or he would have been late for the game. And it's not enough that he has this overwhelming mass of unsaturated fat to share with us, but he also feels that he needs to wave his arms frantically and jump up and down, making his belly look like an aerial video of a 7.2 earthquake.

Now, I know I talk a lot about how difficult it is to be married and have to make compromises, but I think this is a situation where being married can really help. I'm talking to all you fat guys out there. Before you go to the game, get your stomach all painted up and show it to your wife and ask her if she thinks the world wants or needs to see this.

And please, please listen to her answer. Some of us are watching the game with our families, perhaps having dinner in front of the TV. You must stop the madness.

THE LIVING END

I have a theory about the size of a man's butt. (I'm happy to report that I haven't done any research on this.) My theory is that through a man's life, the size of his butt pretty much follows the pattern of the bell curve. It starts out quite small, increases in mass in his early teens, expands exponentially through the thirties and forties, reaches the zenith of its growth potential around the age of fifty-three, and then diminishes in size exponentially until the age of seventy-five, at which time it has returned to being quite small.

I can understand why it enlarges through middle age, because there's usually a fairly substantial gut out front, and if the butt were too small, a man would be unbalanced and unable to stand up. But I don't understand why it has to shrink with age. It seems cruel or at least ironic that when you finally get to the age where you can stop worrying, you've got nothing to fall back on.

RIGHTSIZING YOUR HOME

A lot of people my age are making the move from the two-storey, four-bedroom family home into a one-bedroom condo. They tell me that they want to reduce the work and general hassle of owning and maintaining a house, but I don't believe it. Sure, the condo management people will cut the lawn and shovel the snow and look after the outside maintenance, but they charge you a few hundred bucks a month to do it. Chances are, you could have the same level of service for the same price on your own house. Maintenance is not the issue—it's all about downsizing.

Downsizing is not a new concept. Life does it to most of us. Haven't you ever noticed how much smaller your grandfather is than he used to be? We've been battling life from our four-bedroom fort every day for a lot of years. Now that we're running out of ammo, we need to be a smaller target. Maybe in a condo with security, the world won't bother us as often.

And of course, no extra room means no extra visitors. No matter who drops in, at some point it's going to get late and you're going to have to go to bed and they're going to have to go home. And you will have peace.

That's what this is all about. Moving to a condo is you giving up on conquest and, instead, opting for peace. You've always found peace in the smallest room in the home. Now you're hoping to find it in the smallest home on the block.

LET THERE BE HEADLIGHTS

Take a minute and count the number of headlights on your car. Usually, you come up with the number two, which is not one of my favourites. I like the number eight. With eight headlights, you can have two pointing up, two pointing down, two to the left, and two to the right. The only way another vehicle can surprise you is from the back end, and you can eliminate most of that risk by maintaining a minimum speed of roughly a hundred miles an hour.

So what you have to do is mount six more headlights on the front of your car, in such a way that they are solid yet infinitely adjustable, not to mention waterproof. Sounds like another job for duct tape.

After you've got all the headlights taped to the grill (and make it secure—use lots of tape and run it right back to the doors on each side), aim them as well as you can. They'll need realignment on hot days and after collisions.

You're going to need extra power to run the extra lights, so line up half a dozen car batteries in your back seat. Wire them using metal coat hangers, then attach them to the headlights with two or three sets of jumper cables run from end to end.

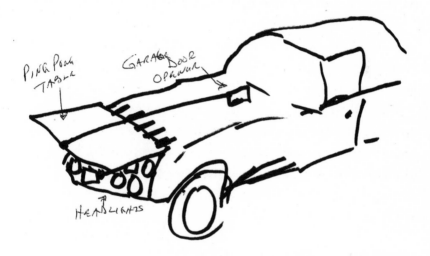

At this point, some of you are probably thinking, "My wife will say it's ugly." Well, if you've got an old garage door opener lying around—and who doesn't?—you can give this a real sporty look. Mount the garage door opener on the hood and attach to it a sheet of plywood (or half a ping-pong table, for those of you who have keys to the community centre). Hinge it with duct tape and now you have a European-style plywood spoiler, giving the effect of hideaway headlights like those you see on Ferraris and Maseratis. If that isn't sharp, then neither am I.

LAST CHANCE

Recently I've been seeing more commercials for wills: how to prepare them, why to have them, what to put in them. I don't think wills are used to their full potential. First of all, you shouldn't try to say how much you care about people in your will. It just makes them feel bad. They don't need to read it from you after you're gone—they need to hear it from you while you're still around.

To me, the true fun is to use your will to make people improve themselves. For example, you can leave your riding mower to your neighbour, providing he returns the hedge clippers he borrowed from you in 1973. (And it has to be the exact pair—you kept a picture.) You can leave your barbecue to the people up the street, providing they camp in your backyard listening to their dog bark all night, as you did for so many years. You can leave five thousand dollars to the city, providing they repave the street like they promised to in the last municipal election. You get the idea. Have some fun with it. A will is your last chance to make a point, and nobody can talk back.

NO POINT

I've noticed that when I ask my computer to do something by pointing at and clicking on an icon, it will try for thirty seconds or so, and then tell me it failed and just go back to where it was. No guilt. No attitude. It doesn't kick anything or hurt itself. I envy that. I'm not like a computer at all. You can't just point and click to make me try something. In fact, the more you point, the less I click. And once I do try something, I don't quit. I just keep working at it until I keel over or the thing I'm working on explodes in a fireball. That's because once I start something, I'd rather get incredibly angry than stop. I have attitude. I kick things. I hurt myself. If my computer could see me, it would say, "You have performed an illegal operation." Maybe one day I'll turn into a computer and everything will be okay. But for that to happen, I'll need a lot more memory.

THE YOUNG AND THE USELESS

Our local television station was doing one of those success profiles of a guy in town who had made a gazillion dollars and had women sending in resumes in hopes of having his children. I found the whole thing mildly irritating at first, but I really lost it when they announced that this guy was twenty-seven years old. No average man over the age of forty needs to hear that. If they can make a V-chip that filters out sex and violence on TV, they should be able to invent a gizmo that prevents the viewer from learning that not only are most people doing better than him but they're also doing it at half his age. Maybe they could even make a thingy that substitutes a higher, more palatable number whenever age is mentioned. Wouldn't it be great to hear that Bill Gates was eighty-seven or Justin Bieber was sixty-three or Sidney Crosby was seventy-four? It would give us all hope for the future.

THE LAST SHALL BE FIRST

I need some computer nerd out there to come up with software that will allow me to scan a contract into my computer, enlarge the fine print, and put it at the top of the document. That would save me a lot of eyestrain and a lot of ink. When my wife said,

"Why do they make the important things so small?" I said it was just nature's way.

HOW TO BUILD A JET-POWERED CAR

Here's a way to reduce your carbon footprint: switch to soapbox derby–style cars. To my way of thinking, we need a smaller, lighter vehicle—one made completely of wood, so it won't rust. Simple but practical. Lightweight with excellent visibility, easy to park, and with room for only one person, which will probably save a few marriages. You steer the vehicle with your feet, which leaves your hands free to use as brakes.

What type of fuel-efficient engine would we use in something like this? I immediately thought of Roman candles, but they wouldn't sell me the quantities I'd need to power this unit. So I suggest we go with fire extinguishers. Point them out the back and attach them to the vehicle using duct tape. All you do is squeeze on the trigger for a blast of carbon dioxide; that will propel you forward to the point where you should be able to maintain thirty miles an hour on a flat road, putting out fires as you go.

On a safety note, I suggest you wear a scarf around your neck, because you're sitting real close to the fire extinguishers and the carbon dioxide gets real cold. You wouldn't want to be cruising down a major thoroughfare with a frozen head.

HOW MEN AND WOMEN WORK

It's always helpful to identify the difference between men and women in the interests of universal peace and global warming. One thing I've noticed is that men and women generally have a different approach to work: women are doers, and men are delegators. Women pride themselves on maximizing their own personal productivity. Men pride themselves on getting someone else to do the job. That's why women are hands-on while men prefer power tools. We're programmed for work avoidance. It's not our fault. The human reproductive process is the model for all other forms of man/woman interaction. The man is there for all the fun and excitement of the first five minutes, and at the end of the meeting, the woman takes sole responsibility for the project for the next nine months.

DRIVING MRS. DAISY

You can tell how long people have been married just by watching them drive their car. Here are a few things I've noticed:

- If he's driving and she's cuddled up close, they're newlyweds. They must also have an old car to be able to sit that close. That proves they're newlyweds as well.

- If she's driving and he's cuddled up close, they've been married for a few years and he's in a little trouble. Alcohol may be involved. Especially if they have bucket seats.
- If he's driving and she's sitting way over on the other side, as far away as she can get, they've been married at least five years and he has forced her to leave the mall before she was ready.
- If he's driving and she's speaking heatedly to him and pointing out directions with her hands, they've been married ten years.
- If he's driving and she's not speaking to him at all, they've been married eleven years.
- If he's driving and she's sitting in the back seat, they've been married fifteen years. If he's wearing a cap, he's also had a serious demotion.
- If they're driving separate cars, they've been married twenty years.
- If she's driving and he's walking, they're divorced.

HOW TO AVOID HAVING YOUR TIME WASTED

I'll try to keep this short. I find that guys my age have a short attention span. I'm not saying that's bad. In fact, most of the time it's a good thing. We're starting to sense that time is running out, and we don't want to waste it reading thick books or watching mini-series or listening to the neighbour talk about her cats. We like short, pithy, meaningful sound bites. People who attempt to communicate with us need to accept that and to alter their style of communication to fit those parameters. Here's a short list of questions I make people ask themselves before they waste my precious time:

- Do I know you?
- Does this information affect me personally, and will not having it cause me bodily harm or, worse still, cost me money?
- Can you express your thought in less than ten seconds?
- Are you planning to use words that I don't know?
- Will you be blocking the exit?

HOW TO SPOT A MIDDLE-AGED MAN'S WALLET

Many of us have several ad hoc time capsules that show the chronology of our lives. Our wallets are one of these. If you found a wallet and it had the following things in it, you'd know it belonged to a middle-aged guy:

- A picture of Charo.
- Ticket stubs from a Herman's Hermits concert.
- A picture of a man in his early twenties wearing the exact same leisure suit that the wallet's owner is currently wearing.
- A large collection of business cards of varying age. They are each from radically different businesses, although they all have the wallet owner's name on them.
- A small calendar identifying the owner's time-share week in Greenland.
- The singed remains of his Ford Pinto proof of ownership.
- A coupon to have his colour done.
- No money.

SENIOR SERVICE

I was in a restaurant for lunch yesterday. It was one of those salad buffet places where you fill your plate with low calorie, no-fat lettuce and tomatoes and then smother it with mounds of creamy salad dressing and a couple of handfuls of bacon bits. So I'm standing at the cashier in a "What a great day" kind of mood, and she says, "Do you get the seniors' discount?" I was so upset, I could barely go back for seconds.

Offering a seniors' discount to people over fifty is a fine incentive for customers and all that, but businesses have got to handle it right. Like most men my age, I think I look about thirty-seven. I don't need some nineteen-year-old sweetie exploding that myth in front of total strangers. Not for a lousy 10 percent. My pride is worth at least 15.

HOW TO MAKE YOUR CAR GO FASTER

It doesn't take magic to make your car go faster. It takes logic and perseverance, and at the lodge, these things are much rarer than magic. The solution is found with physics, not with psychics. So take a few minutes to understand the principles of friction, gravity, and the internal combustion engine.

The Importance of Horsepower

Horsepower is the term for the size of the guns your motor can deliver. It's determined by three things: the size of the engine (displacement), the tightness of the engine (compression), and the explosiveness of the fuel (where are my eyebrows?).

Replace your car's engine with the biggest one you can find.

Big things have big engines—semis, earth movers, trains, cruise ships. Increase the compression by tightening the head bolts with a crescent wrench welded to the end of a flagpole (for extra torque). Wrap the whole engine in duct tape. Use two layers in opposite directions for the tightest seal since MarineLand put vodka in the performance pool.

Now you want a really explosive gas. I suggest jet or rocket fuel, or anything with the numbers 238 after it. Increasing the spark also helps. Try getting a transformer from a nearby hydro pole when the power is off (that last part is important). Wire the transformer between the ignition coil and the distributor. It will raise the voltage from 50,000 volts to 125,000,000,000,000, 000,000,000,000,000,000,000,000,000,000,000,000,000, 000,000,000,000, which will make the car easier to start and give you a more interesting hairstyle. There are ways to get even more horsepower, but I feel they're just too dangerous.

Reducing Friction

While friction is a key component in the propagation of the human race, it is a bad thing in every other race. There are two ways to reduce friction in your car. One is to build the vehicle really well using only the best materials under strict tolerances with stringent quality control. And the other, which is what I tend to favour, is to really lay on the lubricant (see also "Propagation"). A good rule to live by is "If it's dry, something is wrong." That applies to everything except the driver's seat.

Cover everything with lubricant—the shocks, the springs, the linkage, the engine, the driveshaft, the tires, the hood, the windshield, the air freshener, the steering wheel, the door handles, but not the cigarette lighter. A cigarette lighter popping out of your hand can bring an unwanted understanding of the term "grease fire."

DEALING WITH GRAVITY

It's really difficult to reduce gravity. Even in the deepest valley, there is still enough gravity to get a person down and keep him there. So you're better off getting gravity to work for you.

When you're climbing a hill, you're fighting gravity, so don't try to go fast. Why waste the gas? Just go ten or fifteen miles over the speed limit. But when you come over the crest of the hill and start heading down, that, my friend, is a different story. Lay the coals to her. Put both feet on the accelerator and wind her right out. As long as you can focus with either eye, you're not going the maximum.

Einstein said that as you approach the speed of light, time will slow down. So if you're running late, you'll make up time this way. Einstein also said that when you get moving fast enough, distances shrink. So you can squeeze your car in between two trucks. Unfortunately, Einstein proved that there are problems as you reach the speed of light as well, because you will have infinite mass. Which can cut into the mileage. You'll probably notice that when you reach around the twelve-hundred-pound mark, you have no neck and your gut starts honking the horn. That's a good time to ease off on the gas pedal.

And don't worry about the cops. Radar guns can't register the speeds you'll be hitting, and most policemen are hesitant to flag down any vehicle coming toward them at over five hundred miles per hour. Especially if you've just dropped the cigarette lighter.

The most important element is common sense. There's no point in going really, really fast if there are other cars or pedestrians or farm animals in the vicinity. Driving fast can be fun and safe, but not if you do it. Driving fast is for normal people. The fact that you're reading this book disqualifies you.

MY STOMACH IS KILLING ME (and Vice Versa)

I find that a lot of guys my age have trouble with their stomachs. What was once a low-priority and relatively maintenance-free part of their anatomy is now looming large, both physically and medically. I think the main problem is that most of us have no knowledge of or respect for how the stomach works. Here's my take on it: the stomach is where the food is mixed with chemicals that will break it down so the body can burn it. In other words, the stomach is the carburetor of the body. It's not the fuel injector. It can't handle high-quantity intake, no matter how big a super-charger your mouth is. And then there's the quality issue. You can't run a high-performance engine—that is, the human body—on chili dogs and draft beer.

Once in a while you need to fill up on high test (i.e., roughage), something that will get you up and moving, at least during the halftime show. But the biggest problem with the stomach is that it's connected to the brain. If your mind is upset, your stomach will be too. To calm it, you must deal with whatever is troubling your mind, rather than assaulting your stomach with deep-fried jalapenos hoping that will do the trick.

HITTING BOTTOM IN THE TOP DRAWER

I had an unsettling revelation as I was getting dressed the other day. There was some new underwear in my drawer, still in the package. My wife had bought it for me. It's something she does once in a while. And I don't know why, but I tried to think back to the last time I bought my own underwear. It was definitely before I got married. And in the period between high school and my wedding, I just made do with what I had. I didn't buy any in high school either. Or in elementary school. And I didn't buy any before kindergarten, when I was a rookie in the underwear department. And before that, I was in diapers. So the horrible truth hit me: I HAVE NEVER IN MY WHOLE LIFE BOUGHT MY OWN UNDERWEAR!

I don't know what that means, but I suspect it is somehow at the root of so many other problems in my life. If there is anybody out there in the same situation, perhaps we should get together and form a support group. Of course, if we could provide our own support, none of this would be necessary.

TEN SIGNS THAT YOU'RE READY TO RETIRE

1) You have toys in your desk.
2) You carry your golf clubs in the back of your company vehicle (an ambulance).
3) You have lost your appetite for debt.
4) Lately you've been buying a lot of slippers.
5) You're dyeing your hair to make yourself look older.
6) You leave work by 3:30 so you can take advantage of the early bird special.
7) You tell your boss how much better the new guy is at doing your job.
8) You're obsessed with your lawn.
9) Your briefcase is full of brochures from Sarasota.
10) You tried on a pair of pink pants with a white belt and thought they looked sharp.

TOY BOYS

I've spent most of my life at first acknowledging and then foolishly trying to identify the differences between men and women. And I think a big one is in their attitude toward toys.

While both sexes may agree that toys are childish with no redeeming social value, women somehow see that as a bad thing. Or maybe it's the manufacturers' fault. They don't make toys for girls who are past puberty. With men, the process accelerates and the toys get bigger—speedboats, monster trucks, ATVs, radio-controlled cars and planes, bulldozers, nuclear missiles, etc.

Look around at the stores in your city. How many of them carry toys for women? I'm guessing there aren't any, except maybe Chippendales. That's just not fair. In fact, it's sexism at its worst. I say the time has come to give women equal opportunity to be convinced of the value of toys. Then maybe my wife will let me buy that big screen.

KEEP YOUR CREATIVITY TO YOURSELF

With the increasing amount of leisure time available to middle-aged couples over the past few years, we've all started to expand our interests and hobbies. Women are quilting and doing needlepoint and painting in acrylics and making dried floral arrangements. Men are doing woodwork and building model airplanes and renovating unused bedrooms and making lawn ornaments. And all this work is creating a real problem.

Unfortunately, very few of us are any good at this stuff. What we end up with is some butt-ugly thing that they make better with a machine in Taiwan for about ninety-nine cents. But if it was made by your spouse, you can't throw it in the garbage without starting the Third World War.

Some people give their creations to their friends, but there's a risk of them returning the favour. So I say that the government needs to set up designated hobby centres in abandoned schools or whatever. We can all go there on a Saturday morning and do our hobby thing—build or sew or paint—and then when we're finished—and this is the important part—the thing we've made is NOT ALLOWED TO LEAVE THE BUILDING . . . EVER.

HOW TO FIND YOUR TRUE AGE

I read about some guy on the Internet who has different ways of determining your true age. I think it's a formula based on your heart rate and blood pressure and weight and whatever. He himself is over fifty chronologically but is actually only 38.6 on this new measurement system. I think if you go to his website, you must already be at least forty. Young people aren't concerned about their true age unless they get caught in a bar. But I've come up with other ways to measure a person's true age, with some amazing results.

- Alcohol intake: Doctors say you should take in only two alcoholic drinks per day. At that rate, my uncle Ralph is 173 years old.
- Hair loss: On average, men have experienced a 50 percent hair loss by the age of forty and a 70 percent hair loss by the age of sixty-five. By this measurement, the boxing promoter Don King is eleven.
- Waist measurement: A person's girth increases by 2.5 centimetres (1 inch) every decade. This means I age by fifteen years each Christmas.

- Favourite TV shows: Since viewers relate best to people of their own generation, a person's true age is reflected in the TV shows he or she watches. If you watch <u>South Park</u>, your true age is nine. If you watch <u>Jersey Shore</u>, your true age is 36D. If you watch <u>Lawrence Welk</u>, you are reincarnated.

NEW YEAR, SAME OLD YOU

By now, you've broken all your New Year's resolutions and are feeling bad about it. Well, don't. Just think how much worse off you'd be if you hadn't dieted for that whole week or quit drinking for that day. So don't beat yourself up for coming back to the same old you. The medical community will tell you when it's time for you to change.

HOW TO BUILD YOUR OWN TANK

There is nothing more embarrassing than getting your car stuck in a ditch somewhere. Well, there is one thing more embarrassing, but usually you can count on your wife not to blab. Anyway, I've decided to show those of you who don't have paved driveways how you can make your car less vulnerable to sinkholes, mudslides, avalanches, and quicksand.

To go where angels fear to tread, you need one hell of a tread—a tank tread. That's right, just turn your car into a tank. To do it, you're going to need a roll of snow fence, a pair of metal snips, and an axe. This idea is so simple you'll wonder why you didn't think of it a long time ago.

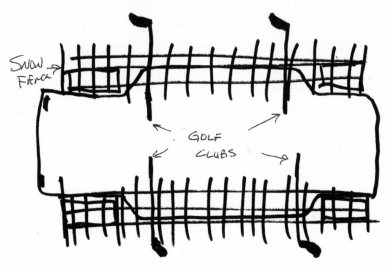

OVERHEAD VIEW

SNOW FENCE

GOLF CLUBS

The first step is to disconnect the emergency brake from the left side of your vehicle. That's what the snips are for. If you're not sure which cable it is, cut them all. Who cares about safety? You're building a tank.

Now the emergency brake will stop only the right-side wheels. To balance that out, disconnect your regular brake lines from the right side of the car so they stop only the left-side wheels. Just take a wrench and disconnect them at the wheel cylinders. If they're rusted on, keep kicking until something breaks. (Toes don't need a cast anyway.)

Now, to give our tank treads room to move freely around the wheels, you have to remove the front half of the front fender and the rear half of the rear fender, which you can do easily with a chainsaw. (Don't use your own chainsaw.) Once that's done, you're ready for your tank tread, which you can buy through an army surplus magazine or make yourself from an old escalator. Or if you're not made of money, just use a piece of snow fence. It's twice as wide as you need, so just cut her in half and you'll have a track for each side of your vehicle.

Mount golf clubs on the roof with duct tape. These will work as guides to keep the treads in line with the wheels. Have the handles attached to the roof so the heads are out to the sides. For long trips use your driver; for short runs the putter is appropriate.

Now you're ready to roll. Driving the tank couldn't be easier. When you want to turn left, you step on the brake. When you want to turn right, you pull on the emergency brake. You can go anywhere. From now on, you don't need a map of where you're going, just the coordinates.

YOUR LUCK CHANGES

Looking back over the years, I notice how the phrase "getting lucky" has changed its meaning. When I was a little boy, "getting Lucky" meant retrieving my dog from the neighbour's patio party. After puberty, the phrase took on a whole new definition. The teen years are in fact the golden era of getting lucky. From there, "getting lucky" referred to my first successful job application, then my first mortgage application, then surviving that tax audit, and then avoiding the axe during the company downsizing. Nowadays, "getting lucky" means the medical tests came back negative.

A ROOM OF HIS OWN

A lot of guys my age have somewhere they can go to be alone and have peace and think and tinker around or whatever. Sometimes it's a club or a bowling alley or a bar. More often it's a place in their own home, such as a basement workshop or a garden shed. But usually, it's the garage. A guy'll have an old couch and a TV and a beer fridge in his garage. It's a place that's all his. A place where he can do and say whatever he wants, and more important, eat and drink whatever he wants. And if there's a lawn mower lying there in fifty or sixty pieces with no hope of ever being reassembled . . . well, that's nobody's business.

Compared to the intimidating environment of the house itself, with the designer furniture and the fancy drapes and the expensive carpets, the garage is pure comfort and relaxation. You can sit anywhere in dirty clothes and put your feet up. You are the master of your environment, instead of vice versa. So to the rest of the family: don't worry about Dad spending time out there in the garage. You know where he is. You know there's only so much trouble he can get into. He's there if you need him. And he will eventually come back into the house a much happier man.

WORK AT BEING A RETIREE

I often hear about guys who worked all their lives to save up for their retirement, and then when they do finally get the golden handshake, they keel over in the first year. The most common theory is that men have a problem adjusting to suddenly having nothing to do, and that the secret to a successful retirement is to keep busy, maintaining an active schedule and having real responsibilities.

I don't agree. That sounds to me like you're supposed to solve the problem by making retirement more like work. I prefer to go the other way, making work more like retirement.

Once you hit the age of forty, take one afternoon a week off work and go sit in the park. When you have a meeting, don't make any suggestions or comments, and when you're asked for an opinion, just shrug. Come in late and leave early. Never answer your phone. Read novels at your desk. Avoid responsibility. You may take some flack, but when your retirement comes up—and it may happen sooner than you expect—you'll be ready.

STAYING GREY

I have a couple of friends my age appearing in big network television shows, and they've each had to dye their hair to keep their jobs. Apparently the television execs don't think the audience can stand to see a grey-haired man on a primetime series. Maybe it's because these execs are twenty-three years old and don't want men who look like their dads to be stars. But what a horrible message it sends to those of us who have grey hair.

Is it over for us? Will it come back with a bottle of Grecian Formula? I'm not sure that would work for me. My face and hair are roughly the same age, so they kind of go together. I wouldn't look right with Russell Brand's hair, and he wouldn't look right with my face.

When I look at myself in the mirror, I kind of think this is the way God wanted me to look, and if it's good enough for him, it's okay with me. But God doesn't run the TV networks. That becomes more obvious every season.

THE LANGUAGE OF TRUNKS

You can pretty much tell how old a driver is by examining the contents of his trunk.

- Spare tire–over thirty
- Spare tire with air in it–over fifty
- Sleeping bag–under twenty
- Sleeping bag for sleeping–over sixty
- Laundry–single, over twenty
- Clean laundry–recently separated, over forty
- Snow shovel–over thirty
- Snowblower–over fifty
- Bag of sand–over twenty
- Bag of Viagra–over seventy
- Body bag–over and out

MIXED MESSAGES

Life is so much more difficult because of the conflicting messages that bombard us throughout each day. And the frequency of these messages has a great impact on our decision-making process. If you get bad advice ten times more often than good advice, your chances of making the right decision are extremely remote.

The recommendations I get in church on Sunday morning are in direct conflict with the ones I get from the bartender and his able-bodied assistants on Monday through Saturday. And church doesn't have a happy hour. You get the same ratio from TV commercials. For every one promoting diet and fitness, there are a hundred pushing burgers and fries. What chance do we have against these kinds of odds? Maybe that's what happens to the president. Maybe he's got one guy telling him to do the right thing and a hundred others advising him that it's business as usual.

So here's an easy solution that we can all live by: listen to everybody's opinions but take your own advice.

BRIGHT IDEA

Now that I've got a lot more white hair in my beard and a lot less of any coloured hair on my head, I can't help noticing that people look at me differently. I know what they're doing. They're pigeonholing me. Stereotyping me. Classifying me as a burnt-out old guy who should be dead soon. Maybe I'm over-sensitive, but I resent that.

I had a guy tailgating me because I was driving pretty slowly in the passing lane. I like the passing lane. No ramps. No trucks. And I'm closer to oncoming traffic, which helps keep me awake. Finally this guy swings around and passes me on the right, and as he does, he looks over at me to express some type of four-letter critique of my driving. But then he sees my old face and makes a gesture that says, "I should have known it would be an old guy." That bugged me, so here's what I decided: Think of your self-image as a flash-light. Think of other people's opinion of you as another flashlight. If their flashlight is brighter than yours, you have a problem.

I'm working hard to make sure that doesn't happen to me. I hope I don't run out of batteries.

HOW TO BUILD A REVERSIBLE CAR

Remember rear-engine cars? The Volkswagen Beetle? Or the Chevy Corvair? You didn't need to be speeding to get a thrill out of one of those, especially the Corvair. That car was unsafe at any speed. But let's drive down memory lane by turning a front-engined/front-wheel-drive car into a rear-engined/rear-wheel-drive classic.

If you think you have to take the engine and all the peripheral equipment out and remount it in the trunk, think again. All you have to do is reverse the interior: turn the seats around, move the dashboard to the back, and rewire the controls.

To remove the seats, you'll need some tools and some oil, or else just a big hammer and an attitude. I prefer attitude to tools. I lose tools.

Once you've removed the seats and the old upholstery, which you wanted to replace anyway, open the hatchback and mount the driver's seat facing backwards. It has to be held in place by bolts or heavy clamps, or if you're thinking like me, duct tape. (A tip: duct tape makes great car upholstery. Install it sticky side out and you won't need seat belts.)

Now, rather than moving all the controls to the back, connect them to a second set of controls from a boat. It should be a boat you no longer want, or one someone you know no longer wants, especially when he finds out it doesn't have controls in it anymore.

Rig the boat's steering wheel to the car's steering wheel and the boat's hand throttle to the car's gas pedal. And for the car's brake pedal, use the anchor rope.

The only remaining problem is that the white headlights are at the back and the red tail lights are up front. Easy to fix with a large screwdriver. Take the screwdriver and smash the red lenses of the tail lights. Then go around the back (formerly the front) and turn the headlights into tail lights by clipping red plastic bowls over them.

It's just that easy to turn a front-engined/front-wheel-drive car into a rear-engined/rear-wheel-drive car. This is the best of both worlds. Looks like a car and drives like a boat (the *Titanic*).

TOO OLD TO BE LOOSE

I was sitting in a train station last week and saw, over in a corner of the waiting area, a couple of teenagers sleeping on the floor.

They were using coats as blankets and backpacks as pillows. And nobody was bothering them or even making comments. It was just accepted that these were a couple of normal sleep-deprived kids off to see the world. But I couldn't help wondering what the response would be if they were middle-aged men, rather than teenagers. I'm guessing not good. Society doesn't approve of men sleeping on the floor in a public place. Not even married men. It's a question of leeway. As we get older, our leeway shrinks. A teenager with the crotch of his pants down around his knees is a hip-hop happening. When a middle-aged man does it, it's a citizen's arrest. Try to imagine a middle-aged guy hitchhiking. Or caddying. Or dating your daughter. There's no leeway.

LOCATION, LOCATION, LOCATION

My whole life can be traced by people and places I wanted to live close to. As a kid, I wanted to live close to the playground. Then I wanted to live close to the friends I made at the playground. Then my girlfriend. Then the tavern. Then my job. Then my kids' school. Then the golf course. Then the doctor's office. Now the hospital. And finally, the funeral home. (I'm counting on a big turnout.)

I THINK, THEREFORE I AM A WOMAN

My wife and I had a little disagreement the other night, and afterward, I was sitting out in the garage trying to figure out where we went wrong. I decided it was during the Industrial Revolution.

Up until then, men and women were on a pretty equal footing. Men worked in the fields while women worked in the home. After the big I.R., the women still worked in the home, but the men were now working in mines and factories. This was a huge setback. When you're working in the fields or in the home, you can think about things. Doing the laundry or bringing in the sheaves are jobs that don't require much of your mind, so you can be forming theories or examining relationships while you're working. But when you're setting off a dynamite charge or working with a two-hundred-ton punch press, you'd better give the task your full attention.

That's why during the Industrial Revolution, men stopped thinking. At first it was just a work thing, so they could keep their fingers. But eventually it permeated all phases of their lives. Meanwhile, women just kept thinking and thinking. And by the time we hit the twentieth century, women had been thinking for so long that they couldn't stop—whereas for men the exact opposite was true.

THE AGE OF SPECIALIZATION

Many experts advise us to fight the aging process. They say we need a disciplined diet and a rigorous exercise regimen, and that will somehow keep us young. This to me is fighting the fundamental laws of nature. The world does not need you to stay young. We have young people who are much more willing and able to do that job. So instead of trying to take the place of a younger, healthier person, why don't you try to find the place that has been reserved for you?

You can find that place by looking at yourself and focusing on your strengths. You may not hear very well, and that's nature's way of telling you to listen more. You may not see very well, and that is nature's way of telling you not to look. You may have lost a lot of strength and speed, which is nature's way of telling you to sit down before you kill yourself. Maybe you could even cheer somebody else on.

Your memory is fading, which is nature's way of preventing you from holding a grudge. Sure, you're getting older, but you can also get better. You just can't get younger. Step away from those Rollerblades. Now.

TEN EXPRESSIONS THAT GIVE AWAY YOUR AGE

1) Groovy.
2) Lucky Strike means fine tobacco.
3) You got it, Pontiac.
4) Far out.
5) Avon calling.
6) Make my day.
7) Book 'em, Danno.
8) To the moon, Alice.
9) What's your sign?
10) I think the president is telling the truth.

HOW TO TELL WHEN YOU'RE TOO OLD TO HAVE CHILDREN

Don't let fertility fool you. Just because you're still capable of producing offspring, that doesn't mean you should. Here are the signs that it's time to hang up your guns:

- You hate all noise that you're not making.
- You don't want to explain anything.
- You think the next diaper that comes into your life should be yours.
- A mid-life crisis and a minivan are not compatible.
- You don't want to spend any part of your golden years at a parent-teacher meeting.
- None of the rooms in your home would look better with Fisher-Price accents.
- Whatever strength is left in your back, you're reserving it for beer cases.
- From here on out, you want to be the centre of attention.

BIG IS BEAUTIFUL

I guess the Space Age is to blame for the worldwide desire for miniaturization. Scientists can get the entire encyclopedia on the head of a pin or something. And everything from phones to cameras to cars is getting smaller. Can we just stop and think about this for a minute? I don't want things to get smaller. When things get small, I lose them. Some days I can't even find my car keys, so can you imagine me trying to locate a pin that has the encyclopedia on it? I think they're just making things smaller so we can fit more useless technology into our homes. I say we go the other way: maximization. Give me a wall-sized TV screen, a great big clunky phone, and a two-foot-thick phone book in an eighteen-point font.

OLD FRIENDS SAVE TIME

When I was younger, I would make friends easily and drop them the same way. I was easy-going then. Not so judgmental. And anybody who says otherwise is a moron. But now that I'm a little more experienced—or "previously enjoyed," as the used luxury car salesmen say—I've changed my whole approach toward friends. At my age, I don't want to make new friends. I want to keep the old ones.

With the old friends, I don't have to waste precious time explaining things like how I got that scar or why I'm not allowed to cross the border. In Hollywood, they call it backstory. I don't have the time or energy to go through my backstory. I want to be with friends who already know it and are sick of hearing about it, and who would rather pretend to have forgiven me for it than force me to bring it up. And I know a few embarrassing things about them too, so it's a level playing field.

My advice is that if you have old friends, stick with them. They are a great source of comfort for the rest of the trip. And the fact that somebody who has known you for a long period of time still finds you tolerable is both a great compliment and flies in the face of many of your wife's theories.

E IS FOR ENOUGH

I know I've been somewhat critical of technology from time to time, but when it comes to email, all is forgiven. Email is the greatest form of communication since the wink. It's quick, it's effortless, it's free, and you don't have to lick anything. There is no better way to contact people, even your mother.

For one thing, email is undaunting. It's a small space to fill. By the time you say hello and mention the weather and your bursitis, you only have room left to say goodbye. And it's the best part of communication—the transmitting part. It's every man's dream: a one-way conversation.

Sure, people can email you back, but you can delete those messages without reading them. Is this a great thing or what? If any of you disagree with this, please send me your comments. My email address is likeIcare@I'llgetrightonthat.com.

ALL OUR TOMORROWS

We have a tendency as we get older to spend too much time looking back. It's natural. When you're older, your life is like looking at yourself naked in a mirror: the biggest part is behind you. A little reminiscing is okay, but you're better off staying focused on the future. And the shorter it is, the more attention you should pay to it. The trick is to stay optimistic, so here's a list of things you can look forward to in your declining years:

- People aren't going to ask you to help them move.
- Friends will stop trying to set you up with their sisters.
- Life insurance salesmen will stop calling.
- Product warranties will become less of a concern.
- People will assume that the young woman who visits you is a nurse.
- You can stop trying to lose weight.
- You can be the centre of attention by always taking your will to family gatherings.

SUCCESS SUCKS

Here's the thing that's bad about successful people: they tend to be successful in most things they do. If they're good at running a business, they're probably good at running a family too. Congratulations to them and everything, but the last thing you need is to spend time with a person who not only makes ten times your annual salary but also gets along better with his kids. And no matter how much you think you get along with that successful guy, somewhere deep down inside, each of you is thinking, "What a dink."

THE SURPRISING NUTRITIONAL VALUE OF JUNK FOOD

When I was a kid, there was no such thing as health food because back then all food was pretty healthy. Today, thanks to breakthroughs in technology, we can eat a three-course meal that is about 2,394 steps removed from a farm. In fact, many of our modern snack foods are byproducts from the manufacturing of synthetic upholstery.

Generally speaking, a fast food snack with a name like Cheez-O-Rinos has virtually nothing to do with cheese. Some consumers feel this is false advertising, but in fact, the list of ingredients on the package quite clearly includes "cheez," not "cheese." What's not mentioned is that "cheez" is an industrial term for a waste chemical that's skimmed off vats of latex house paint.

When you check the nutritional value of snacks like Cinnamon Whizzeys, Choco-Drips, or Gribble Grabble, you'll find that the label on the cellophane package usually says something like this: "Each 10 oz. serving contains the recommended annual intake of salt, vitamin L, and di-ethyl-methyl-ketone. Uranium has been added to preserve freshness."

If you are going to hoover down a lot of junk food, your heart certainly doesn't deserve the extra strain that comes from worrying about what you've just inhaled. So when some health nut teases you because you've just knocked back a party-size bag of ketchup-flavoured Tater-rinos and a gallon of Zap cola for breakfast, pull out this handy chart, which proves that snack foods are good, and good for you.

Snack Food	Why It's Good For You
Pretzels – – – – – –	Pretzels are an excellent source of fibre and salt. Also, they're shaped for getting between teeth to clean them.
Sour cream and onion potato chips – –	This snack is basically a complete well-balanced meal. It includes the four basic food groups: 1. dairy (sour cream); 2. fruit and veg (onions); 3. grains (potatoes); 4. meat (the little bits of green stuff).
Boston cream doughnuts – – – – –	This is another well-balanced food. The custardy-yellow centre provides you with the recommended daily intake of dairy and sugar. If it's artificial, then you're getting soybean oil, which is also good for you. The doughnut fills you with fibre and sugar, while the chocolate glaze gives you sugar and energy. And if it's a sugar doughnut, it gives you extra energy and extra sugar.

French fries with gravy and ketchup – –	Recommended for those who don't always get enough vegetables. The fries are potatoes; the ketchup is made of two kinds of vegetables— tomatoes and sugar cane; and the gravy is basically vegetable oil or soybean oil. The thicker gravy is rich in vitamins and ribald-flavin.
Jelly beans – – – – –	Another great source of energy. The red food colouring helps keep your complexion looking pink, while the hard candy coating is essential for strong nails and shiny hair. A big bowl of green jelly beans is as good for you as a big bowl of green beans.
Pez – – – – – – –	Pez candies build strong bones. And loading them into the dispenser develops fine motor skills and hand– eye coordination.
Chewing gum – – – –	Gum builds strong jaw muscles, cleans bits of potato chips from your teeth, and freshens your breath. The little Bazooka Joe comic encourages literacy among our young people.

BE A GOOD MIXER

I'm not sure exactly when I figured out that people are made up of chemicals, but my guess would be sometime in the 1960s. We are all complex mixtures of various chemicals. A change in the chemicals makes a change in the person. Hydrogen and oxygen make water. That's it. Anything you add to that combination makes a huge difference. You can't also throw in a boatload of Bunker C Crude and still have water, as everyone at BP now knows. So we should all be aware of the chemicals we put in our bodies every day.

The more chemicals, the more chemical reactions. The more chemical reactions, the less chance you have of making new friends or being allowed back into the hot tub. You'll need to do a lot of your own research on this because everyone's different, but as a general rule, you should never mix carbonated overproof alcoholic fruit drinks with any type of cheese derivative having a pH above 9.

THINGS YOU CAN NOW SAY

As the years go by, an unwritten law allows you privileges that you've never had before. While you may not be able to *do* as many things as you used to, you can now *say* more stuff than you ever could. Here is a list of expressions that are acceptable once you hit mid-life and beyond:

- These days, there's too much sex in everything. Except my life.
- Tell the waiter to bring me something soft.
- You're both sitting in my chair.
- We were the first family on our street to have a television.
- We were the first family on our street to have a radio.
- We were the first family on our street.

THE RULE OF THUMB

I've been a husband for most of my adult life, and certainly for all of my mature adult life, and I've watched the marriage evolve over that period of time. I've found that the average married woman regards her husband as some strange life form who means well but basically doesn't get it. He becomes an obstacle to a quiet, easy, stress-free life. Someone who has to be cajoled and coaxed and tricked into doing things like shopping or having the relatives over.

I'd just like to point out that the role of being the opposition is a valuable one that is reflected in court procedures and parliamentary government. Husbands are the opposable thumbs of relationships. There is an implied mutual dependency, as the contrary positions of husband and wife make both stronger and more effective. Without husbands, the wives would simply be four fingers waving in the breeze, and without wives, husbands would just be a thumb hitchhiking its way through life.

HOW TO MAKE A TOBOGGAN

If you're like me, you have more than once found yourself driving down the highway when all of a sudden your car hood flies up and blows off. Don't you hate that? Probably my own fault for closing the hood with the same piece of duct tape over and over. But let me tell you, it's worth going back to get that hood, even if you have to apologize to the people at the bus stop. That hood can save you thirty bucks come Christmas, because with a little skill and ingenuity—and some rope—you can turn it into a toboggan.

The first step is to put the rope through the front of the hood and tie it to something so it doesn't flop around when you're coming down the hill. Or get the fat kid to sit on it.

Now, you don't just want to ride your hood/toboggan by sitting down on the bare metal. You need to be a little higher so you can see what's up ahead, 'cause there's nothing worse than screaming down a farmer's hill and getting hit in the face with a frozen trail treat.

Remove the front seat from a former friend's car (he shouldn't be driving in winter anyway) and strap it to the inverted hood with duct tape. Now go out and have yourself some fun. And make sure you really enjoy that first run, because this unit comes in at around four hundred pounds, and you may not be able to convince your wife to drag it back up the hill.

HOW TO AVOID BEING REMINDED OF YOUR AGE

You've taken steps so you won't be reminded that you're getting older. You avoid mirrors and brightly lit rooms and anyone who knows your true age, but there are physical activities you should also stay away from. If you want to maintain that healthy, young self-image, pay attention to the following:

- If you drop something, don't bend over. If you can't pick it up with your toes, write it off.
- Don't run. People will forgive your tardiness much more readily than your red face, your heavy breathing, or the fact that your stomach is still bouncing.
- Don't get into any vehicle that's short enough for you to see over. You may never get out.
- Don't wear tight clothing or stand in the wind. Keep your shape a mystery.
- Don't dance. You don't know any modern steps, you can't hear the music all that well, and songs are a lot longer than they used to be.

THERE'S A REASON YOU'RE OUT OF TOUCH

I saw another "long-lost brother reunion" thing on one of those talk shows for people who tell their whole family to shut up so they can watch a television program on communicating. On this particular episode, a brother and sister were brought back together after twenty years of no contact. Now, it was a touching scene when they hugged each other and shed a tear or two, but I had a sense that this was all a huge invasion of privacy.

We've got the Internet and the phone book and there are only ever six degrees of separation, so I have to believe that any two people who want to find each other do. When you see a reunion, that can only mean the person who wanted to do the finding did a way better job than the person who wanted to do the hiding. It looks good for a few minutes on television, but an hour later, I'll bet somebody is saying, "By the way, you still owe me money/an apology/both."

So if there's anybody out there trying to reunite with somebody, accept that the reason you can't find the person is because he or she doesn't want to meet you halfway. Focus instead on the people who've been with you all the way along. Unless you owe them money or an apology or both.

SOME ASSEMBLY REQUIRED

My wife bought a computer desk this week in the form of two boxes sticking out of the car trunk, each of which outweighed me. I wrestled them into the living room and tried to open the boxes carefully, but I'm not at my best when something heavy has just fallen on my foot. Inside were a couple of dozen slabs of fake wood, five bags of hardware, and a twenty-seven-page instruction manual. I learned to read manuals last summer after I assembled what I thought was a five-speed bicycle and turned out to be a wheelbarrow. Three days and a bunch of repeated steps later, the desk was together.

So now I'm thinking, "What if we don't like it and want to take it back?" I've already scratched it and wrecked the box, and I'd have to take it apart just to get it into the car. And it struck me then that unassembled furniture is like a marriage. It may not be perfect, but when you think about the hassle of taking it back, you stick it in the corner and try not to look at it too closely.

YOUR RIDE ENDS HERE

We have laws in this country that say once you reach the age of eighty, you have to have a driver's test every year. A lot of men dread it because they know that'll be the end of their driving career. The truth is, most driving careers should end long before they get that far. I see middle-aged people who squinted at the menu in a restaurant walk to their cars and drive home. Right now, the cops pull you over for spot checks to catch drunk drivers and unsafe vehicles, but if the program was expanded to include surprise driving tests, a lot of us would be taking the bus.

Now, I'm not saying you eighty-year-olds are being picked on. I agree you don't drive any worse than the rest of us. But you have been getting away with it for a lot longer. So stop dreading the driver's test. It may give you your best chance to reach eighty-one.

HOW TO TELL IF YOU'VE LOST YOUR PLACE IN THE FOOD CHAIN

We all know we need to save the planet and protect the animals and all that stuff, but once in a while, we also need to remind ourselves of the various priority levels of plant and animal life. Here are a few signs that something is out of whack with nature's pecking order:

- The dog has eaten your lunch.
- You're sleeping on the couch because the cat is on your pillow.
- You can't take a vacation because you can't find anyone to feed the fish.
- You're being fined by the parks department because you allowed a tree to fall on your home.
- You saved so much heating fuel last winter that you contracted pneumonia in the comfort of your own family room.
- You can't go out to a friend's house because your kids have the car.

HE'S GOT YOUR STUPIDITY

I was talking to some friends whose son just did something really stupid. To me that just proves he's not adopted, but they're upset about it.

Now, I know children can get into serious problems as they're growing up, but I think the mistakes and harmless goofy things are just as important. Those foolish mistakes are a great learning experience for them, and it's also a comfort for a parent to know he's not the only goofball in the family. Yes, you want your kids to be successful, but you don't want them to be too successful. It's embarrassing to have a brilliant daughter or a son who's a millionaire. It makes you look like a loser because you couldn't do what she or he did. Or worse yet, it implies that your wife's genes are the ones responsible for your kid's success.

AVOID THE YOUNG

My nephew was complaining to me the other day about his part-time job at a fast food place, where he works indoors for $5.80 an hour and all the saturated fat he can stuff into his fanny pack. I was telling him that when I was a kid, I worked as a milkman's helper out in the freezing cold for a two-dollar bill a day.

He had no idea what I was talking about. He'd never heard of a milkman or seen a two-dollar bill. I'm not even sure he knows what freezing cold is. And I didn't try to educate him because I've been married long enough to know that most things can't be explained. The person either gets it or he doesn't. And it's not his fault. My nephew has just as much trouble trying to tell me what he's learning in school, or why he likes that music, or how much more hardware he's planning to attach to his facial features.

The message is that we should all hang out with our own peer groups. The people of our generation are a lot more likely to understand what we're talking about and forgive us for what we've done. I recommend that you marry someone around your same age, work for a boss from your own era, and always give your side of the story to the cop with the grey hair.

STOMACHING EACH OTHER

I've been married over thirty years, and when people ask me how you can make a relationship last that long, I tell them you have to marry the right person. I compare it to food. Sure, you may like spicy food once in a while, but over the long haul, you're better off with meat and potatoes—something that will sustain you over the years without destroying your body. You need to pick a meat-and-potatoes type of partner. And don't think you can sneak out on occasion for a spicy snack. Your wife can always tell.

WHEN IT'S BETTER NOT TO LAUGH

- When you're meeting your new boss.
- When the judge asks if you'd been drinking that night.
- The first time you see your girlfriend in a bathing suit.
- When the auditor asks if you declared your full income.
- When someone you're hoping to inherit money from drops her teeth.
- When you've just been threatened by members of a motorcycle gang.

- When someone you're married to stubs her toe.
- In church or anywhere that nobody else is laughing.

GIVE ME A BIG EMPTY NEST

They say that as you get older and the kids move out, you're supposed to downsize your house. I don't want to do that. As I age I want more space, not less. My coordination will be down a notch or two and I'll probably have a few more pounds on me, so I need generous doorways with lots of clearance. And I won't be getting out as much as I do now, so the house will be my whole world. I don't want to live in a world whose four corners I can see from anywhere in the living room.

And when you're living in one open room, you have to put your projects away all the time—not to mention explaining the paint stains and burn marks to people who don't understand the handyman mindset. Give me a big house with lots of rooms for my twilight years. Those tiny retirement homes aren't for me. I may think small, but I live big.

WEATHER WISE: AN ARMCHAIR ALMANAC OF WOODLAND WISDOM

Just because you don't have access to a radio, a television, or an Environment Canada satellite downlink, that doesn't mean you have to be at the mercy of the weather. The observant outdoorsperson knows that nature signals approaching trouble, giving those who are weather-wise plenty of time to seek shelter where there's a big chair, beverages, chips, and a cable sports channel. All you have to do is keep an eye out for the following:

Thunderstorm

Distant: Cicadas stop chirping. Sparrows grow quiet. Thin, wispy clouds that look like shredded tube socks appear. Wolves circle, grow agitated. Ants march in straight lines carrying umbrellas.

Imminent: Wolves seek shelter under your bed. The guy you're fishing with looks over your shoulder and says, "Uh-oh." A loud crack! A flash of light! And you wake up in a hospital.

Hailstorm

Ants form into circles. Beavers play poker. Birds grow visibly agitated and are given to unnecessary shoving. Cicadas become verbally abusive.

Snowstorm

Dogs grow nervous and edgy. Squirrels swallow their nuts in fear. Moss seems damp when you stuff it in your pants. Ants start watching NASCAR on television.

Flash Flood

Sparrows stop singing. Ants form into rowing teams. Skunks start wearing life jackets.

Partly Cloudy with Moderate Temperatures and Clearing in the Afternoon

Sparrows stop singing and start rapping. Beavers nervously twiddle their lips. Chickens lay black eggs.

Tornado

Distant: Ants do the hokey-pokey. Cicadas burrow into large hairdos. Dogs grow visibly agitated; cats grow visibly relaxed. Sheep and goats seek shelter in your basement.

Imminent: Low black clouds, high white clouds, and a flying shrub all appear. Cows and horses dig bomb shelters.

Sunny and Clear

Birds fly in circles. Foxes put on suntan lotion. Fish swim upside down. Trees point upward to the sky.

CALL WAITING IS THE HARDEST PART

I was talking to an acquaintance on the phone the other day, and I heard that telltale breakup in his voice that indicated he was getting another call coming in. He ignored it. And then I remembered all the other times people I was talking to got another call and said, "Hang on a minute—I'm getting another call," and left me to go and answer it.

So now I've decided that another person's response to his call waiting is a pretty good indication of your relationship. If he refuses to take the other call no matter what, you're solid. If he waits until the other call interrupts several times or tells you he's expecting an important call and then excuses himself, that's still okay. But if he jumps at the first chance to bail out of talking to you, that can only mean you have no . . . Hang on a minute—I'm getting another call.

HOW TO TELL WHEN THEY DON'T LIKE YOU

It's always good to know where you stand with people, but many of us have difficulty communicating with clarity. So here are a few signs that will tell you when someone really doesn't like you:

- She refuses to make eye contact. Even when you're standing on her foot.
- He tries to sell you Amway stuff.
- When you ask him to drive you home from work, he claims he brought the unicycle that day.
- When you talk to her, she looks like she's having a really big cramp of some kind.
- When he sees you're the only elevator passenger, he waits for the next one.
- She suggests you run for political office.

THE ART OF STIFLING

There's really never a good time to yawn, but we middle-aged married men are frequently faced with really, really bad times to yawn. These almost always involve a spouse who's upset about something we've said or done. We know she's right and we have true remorse, but still, yawns happen. Especially after, say, 8 p.m. Nothing good will happen if you yawn while you're undergoing behaviour modification. You need to learn how to hide a yawn.

I suggest you stand in front of a mirror and practise clenching your teeth really hard without showing any movement of your facial muscles. This may require weight gain, but you should do whatever you have to. Try turning a yawn into a cough. Sometimes that works. Just make sure your mouth is relatively empty. As a last resort, go with the "lookaway," where you turn your head at least 97 degrees and run to the window. When your wife asks what's wrong, hold up your hand to buy enough time to complete the yawn and then say you thought you saw a robin or an alien spacecraft or something.

Of course, the best policy is to make your faux pas early enough in the day that the whole discussion takes place well before the Yawning Hour.

HOW TO GO ICE FISHING

Step One

Do this activity in the winter. No kidding.

Step Two

Learn how to hot-wire a snowmobile.

Step Three

Hot-wire a snowmobile and send the least popular guy out on the lake. Chances are, he will sink through the ice and drop like a stone to the bottom. DO NOT ATTEMPT TO FISH IN THE RESULTANT HOLE. That's important. Instead, go to a different lake before the cops arrive and you waste the whole day explaining what happened.

Step Four

Hot-wire a nicer snowmobile and go out onto a safer lake. Hold up a three-foot length of four-inch pipe and stick the bottom end into the ice. Fill the pipe with gasoline and light it. In no time at all, you will have a four-inch hole in the ice. If you park your snowmobile too close to the burning pipe, you will end up with an even bigger hole and an interesting story to tell all the nurses at the burn unit.

Step Five

Bait your hook and drop it into the hole. Try not to think about your feet until they are completely numb. If you have a chainsaw, you can cut a trough in the ice and troll. Otherwise, you're pretty well limited to jerking the line up and down and letting your mind wander. Do not fight the boredom. It is an intrinsic component of the sport.

Step Six

If you catch anything other than pneumonia, you may need help reeling it in. Especially if it's thicker than four inches. Many of today's sophisticated fishing reels are not meant to be operated with frozen fingers, so thaw your fingers by putting them in your mouth, unless you really don't like the taste of bait. Once you've landed the fish, stick them face down in the snow until frozen. This will eliminate the need for a stringer, because you can mount the fish on Popsicle sticks and throw them into your cooler.

Step Seven

Once you're back to the cabin, cover the fish in a light coating of bread crumbs and butter and then fry them up in a quart and a half of Scotch. Take them out of the pan and feed them to the cat while you drink the broth. This will remove all memory of the outing and allow you to go ice fishing on another occasion.

IT'S NOT HOW GOOD YOU LOOK, IT'S HOW HARD YOU TRY

As we get a little older and lose the blush of youth—and the slimness of youth and the smoothness of youth and the hair of youth and the youngness of youth—we need to recalibrate our instruments before evaluating our level of attractiveness. For most of us over fifty and beyond, it's not fair to be judged on whether we look good. How can we possibly look good? We didn't look good in our prime, and we haven't appreciated over time. Instead, we now need to be judged on how much effort we put into our appearance. Did we shower? Put on fresh clothes? Shave? Get a haircut? Do we smell nice? Women love that.

There's something inspirational about a person who keeps fighting against insurmountable odds. You've seen the photos, you've looked in the mirror, and yet you keep trying. Your partner will recognize these initiatives as attempts to please and will reward you—maybe not with style points, but certainly with effort points. And at our age, that and Miss Congeniality may be all there is.

WHAT NOT TO WEAR

Acceptance is a key component of a happy life. Chances are, your physiology has evolved considerably throughout your adult life. Your senses are probably somewhat less sharp; your patience and perseverance have diminished. And your annual weight increase has outperformed the stock market. All these factors affect your wardrobe:

- Shoes with laces
- Tight jeans and T-shirts, or any other clothes that have nowhere to keep your reading glasses
- Anything stretchy or see-through
- Anything that says "Bay City Rollers" on it
- Anything with buttons smaller than an Oreo
- Anything sleeveless
- Anything with a plunging neckline
- Shorts

TWELVE SIGNS YOU HAVE A BAD MECHANIC (DON'T ASK HOW I KNOW)

1) He charges you a half-hour's labour for opening the hood because he couldn't figure out the latch.
2) You tell him your car is a Ford and he's never heard of it.
3) He opens up your transmission and whistles, then says, "Wow, look at all the little bitty parts in here!"
4) His certified mechanics diploma is written in Magic Marker.
5) He has only one tool: a borrowed sledgehammer.
6) He tries to inflate your flat tire with his mouth.
7) He tries to loosen the wheel nuts by hand and then announces, "These babies are really on here. I'll need a wrench."
8) You mention you had trouble with the dipstick and he fires his helper.
9) He inspects your resonator and announces, "Look, your muffler had a baby!"
10) He tries to replace your oil filter with an air filter, and when it won't fit, he concludes, "This must be metric."

11) He asks lots of questions like a good mechanic should, but one of them is "Where's the engine?"

12) When you drive up to the service bay, he's riding the hoist and yelling, "Geronimo!"

THINK BEFORE YOU RETIRE

These days, a lot of guys are being offered an early retirement package. And most of them are taking it—mainly because their feelings are hurt by a company that, after twenty-five years of service, says, "You're so useless we're offering you a bonus to quit."

I know this can be a difficult time, but before you take an early retirement of any kind, there are a few people you should check with. First, your wife. Is she going to let you mope around in your pajamas watching *Judge Judy*, or is she expecting the laundry done and dinner on the table when she gets home from work? And how do your kids feel about Dad lying on the couch while they're at school? What happens on Career Day, when you come in with a crossword puzzle? How about the city parks department? Do they think their pristine image will be enhanced by your presence on a bench somewhere?

Don't do it. When the bosses offer the early retirement, hold out for a big payday and a transfer to somewhere exotic. If you're useless enough, they might just go for it, and if you're not, they'll keep you.

WORD SEARCH

Here's a puzzle for those quiet evenings when there's nothing on TV because all the professional athletes have gone on strike again. The theme of this word search is different kinds of fish.

Word List

lake trout	hammerhead	muskie	minnows
catfish	walleye	minnow	grouper
rook	sturgeon	smallmouth	turbot
rock bass	pickerel	eels	bass
sunfish	tuna	sharks	angelfish
perch	largemouth	goldfish	kippers
cod	pike	salmon	

```
L A K E T R O U T C A T F I S H R O O K
R O C K B A S S S U N F I S H P E R C H
C O D H A M M E R H E A D W A L L E Y E
S T U R G E O N P I C K E R E L T U N A
L A R G E M O U T H P I K E M U S K I E
M I N N O W S M A L L M O U T H E E L S
S H A R K S G O L D F I S H S A L M O N
M I N N O W S G R O U P E R T U R B O T
B A S S A N G E L F I S H K I P P E R S
```

HOW TO MAKE THE NEIGHBOURS THINK YOU'RE RICH

Perception is everything. Here are a few ways to make your neighbours think you're rich:

- Once a week, arrive home honking the horn, jump out of the car, and pop a champagne cork, then rush inside laughing. (Quickly reinsert the cork so you're ready for next week.)
- Have a set of magnetic signs that you stick on the sides of any trucks parked in front of your house: Excelsior Indoor Pools, Monarch Billiard Tables, Deluxe Home Theatre.
- Once a month, come out of your house with your brief-case handcuffed to your wrist. Look around furtively while your son, dressed as a policeman, escorts you to your car. Speed off.
- Stop at a fancy restaurant and pick up their empty expensive wine bottles to put out in your own recycling box.
- Make a deal with a friend to cut each other's lawns.

NEVER STOP LEARNING

Sometimes at our age, we lose our enthusiasm for new expe-riences because we think we've tried everything or we've lost our confidence or we're tired of standing in line in the emergency department. The trick with things you've never done is to pick something you can actually do. Friends and family may have suggestions. Maybe fly fishing or lawn bowling or origami. My wife suggested I try not interrupting her, but that only led us into an ongoing argument about time and space.

HOW TO BUILD A FIRE TRUCK

Maybe you've always wanted to be in the volunteer fire department but have never joined because you don't have time or can't pass the physical or just don't want to be spending your weekends with the kinds of losers who are attracted to that kind of hobby.

Well, instead of turning normal citizens into firefighters, why don't we just turn a normal car into a fire truck? Who hasn't thrilled to the sight of a huge fire truck roaring down the street to put out a blaze you started totally by accident? It wasn't your fault—it's the lousy instructions that come with electrical appliances.

Fire trucks need shovels, picks, and axes. The trucks carry these tools on the outside, where firefighters can get them in an emergency. So just drill holes in your trunk lid, slightly larger than the diameter of the handles. Then the tools will sit right there, ready for use. Don't worry about the damage to the lid, because you're going to paint this baby fire engine red.

Fire trucks also have lots of flashing lights. And so do you: Christmas lights. You probably have a set hanging off your eaves-trough that you forgot to take down, right? Just hook them to an extension cord. (That will limit the range of your truck, but any fire that's farther away than the length of an extension cord is probably none of your business.) Attach the string of bulbs to your fire truck with wire staples, plastic clips, or duct tape.

A fire truck also needs a siren. Your horn is a good start, but for extra noise, loosen your alternator belt and your fan belt and your power steering belt, and then folks will hear you coming. If you really want to be safe, punch a few holes in the muffler. Plenty of hose is essential too, so get yourself a number of hoses and reels from the hardware store (or borrow them from some-one who's not around), and attach them near the front of the car. You can hook the hoses right to the engine's water pump, and this becomes a pumper truck. And don't worry about them not matching. We're going to paint this baby fire engine red.

A fire truck wouldn't be a fire truck without a ladder that can turn in any direction (because fires can happen in any direction, and you may park in any direction). So for that you need a rotating platform. Hold a three-by-three piece of plywood in the middle of your roof and drive a six-inch spike down through the middle of it. (Make sure no one is in the car when you do this.) To make your pivot point, run a rod through the ends of the ladders and through a couple of screw eyes in the roof, and then run rope up through some pulleys and you'll have a ladder that fights fires in two sepa-rate directions at the exact same time. And she goes up or down, just like the professional units but at a fraction of the cost.

Just a word of caution: don't drive with the ladders in the up position. Personal experience has shown that the ladders will make contact with high-tension wires, and although wood doesn't conduct electricity, it burns well. My fire truck unfortunately caught fire. As soon as it cooled off, I painted it a beautiful fire engine red.

FAIRWAY FRIENDS

I have golfing buddies. They're good guys, and we all get along just fine. But I think if you took those same four guys and put them in a car or sat them at a restaurant table or parked them on a bench for four hours, they would eventually be bickering and entertaining homicidal thoughts. This is because men have trouble socializing with each other when there's nothing else to do. Put them together at a ball game or a racetrack or a golf course and everything's fine.

Women, on the other hand, seem the complete opposite. They've been known to turn off a television in favour of conversation. They often spend a couple of hours over coffee with a friend. They work from a different set of rules than we do. Conversation can never be the central focus for men. None of us has all that much to say, and we have even less interest in hearing what the other guy has on his mind.

That's why golf is such a great game for men. It's the perfect way to feign interest in your friends without wasting a whole afternoon.

UNMAKE YOUR PLANS

Once a year, you really need to clean out your drawers. More important, you have to throw out all your previous day planners. They'll just make you feel stupid and old. I was thumbing through some that I found in the back of my desk. They go back a few years and had some interesting entries, including the following:

- March 12, 1975: Cancel VHS machine. Order Beta instead.
- April 14, 1979: Blow off meeting with Bill Gates.
- June 4, 1995: Buy Bre-X stock.

Get rid of all those day planners right now so that you can get on with your life. The secret to happiness in old age is to erase all traces of personal blunders and let fading memory work its magic. It's called the George Bush Approach.

BRING BACK THE GOLD STAR

Back when I was in elementary school, we had a point system that allowed students to accumulate points over the week and have a shot at going home on Friday with a gold star. I miss that. We need to bring that sense of success back into our lives. Here's a sample list of achievable rewards. Get a hundred points and the gold star is yours.

- Went to work most days: 10 points
- Vacuumed potato chip fallout around La-Z-Boy: 15 points
- Bought flowers for your wife: 20 points
- Bought flowers for somebody else's wife: minus 20 points
- Said no to something illegal, immoral, or fattening: 10 points
- Watched a half-hour of PBS: 10 points
- Looked at your wife when she was talking to you: 15 points

- Listened to your wife when she was talking to you: 25 points
- Loaned money to your adult son: 20 points
- Got money back from your adult son: 0 points
- Had an ache and didn't mention it: 15 points
- Had a surprise for your wife: 10 points
- Had a pleasant surprise for your wife: 50 points

HARDWARE 10, SOFTWARE 2

These days there is a great deal of emphasis placed on communication and interaction. We have cellphones and smartphones and pagers and email and networking. We have all this technology allowing us to exchange ideas easily and instantly. So what are we doing with it? We're calling people when we don't need to. We're programming our cellphones to play tunes instead of ringing. We're getting non-essential messages in a variety of formats. We're playing computer games at our desks with strangers from around the world. We haven't really improved communication—we've just made it easier for bad ideas to be shared.

Before the techno revolution, if you had a theory you presented it to a friend or a colleague first to see if it had merit. You could limit the embarrassment. Now if you have a theory, you create a website and broadcast it to the world. Life gets very difficult when everybody knows you're an idiot. It's bad enough when only your wife knows.

DIDN'T YOU DO SLIGHTLY WELL

I don't think we should feel like failures when we don't have a significant impact on the world. It's often the little things—the small accomplishments, the minor victories—that are the most satisfying.

So for the sake of your own mental health, take a few minutes at the end of each day and try to focus on some tiny breakthrough you had in the past twenty-four hours. Maybe you feel good about not eating that doughnut. Maybe you feel good about eating them all. It doesn't matter what it is. Look for small accomplishments. I consider each day that the police don't have to come to my home a true blessing.

Find ways to feel good about yourself. We can't all be Nelson Mandela or Albert Einstein or Jerry Springer.

WATCH THAT TELEVISION

You're on the couch watching TV, grazing the dial with your thumb and tapping the remote like you're sending Morse code.

Phase One

Your wife asks you to stop doing that and just find something and stay with it. You reply that you can't decide what to watch until you find out what's on. And you say it all without taking your eyes off the set.

Phase Two

Your wife suggests you look at the guide on the TV, which is what it's for.

Phase Three

Your wife picks up her knitting or a book. Finally you settle on what you want to watch—a comedy, a sports event, and something with guns—and you're keeping yourself apprised of what's going on in all three. Then something really good happens on the comedy. Like Hawkeye is going to get a girl for Radar. So you settle on it for a while. Your wife looks up, but just then the commercials start and you're back on the road, thumbing your way to a better show.

Phase Four

Your wife gets up, exits the room, goes out and buys her own TV, and files for divorce. It can happen. Life is about choices. So is television. You can't have a successful marriage and a TV remote. I say go for the successful marriage.

Unless the playoffs are on.

THEREFORE I AM NOT THINKING

Thinking is usually a good thing. It can save you from physical harm and psychological damage. But thinking at the wrong time can also create a lot of problems. Here is a short list of times when it's better not to think:

- When you're being rolled in for surgery.
- When you're being disciplined by a loved one.
- When you're watching an approaching hockey puck.
- When you're undergoing a tax audit.
- When you're at a wrestling match.
- When you're getting directions.

- When you're assembling an explosive device.
- When your spouse is telling you what to wear.
- When you're asked for an opinion.
- When you're at a board meeting.
- Whenever you're feeling smart.

THE END IS NOT NIGH

I heard on the news that one day over the next few months, several of the planets are going to align themselves with Mars (which I think was a hit for the Fifth Dimension). It occurred to me that some cult leader is going to predict that day will be the end of the world. And he's going to say that we should all prepare.

I'm not exactly sure what that means. I wouldn't know what to pack for a world termination. I guess something loose-fitting and some sensible shoes. Okay, that's a little glib, but I don't honestly think the world-ending thing is going to happen. So instead of expecting the rest of us to prepare for the world to end, I suggest these fanatics prepare for the world not to end. What then? What if we hit the stroke of midnight and there's no horrific conflagration? Don't you think they should prepare for that? Maybe it's time to engage in a new activity. Might I humbly suggest rational thought?

IT TAKES A TROUBLED MAN

I don't know whether this is a male thing, but I find I do my best work and make my best efforts when I'm in trouble. When everything's going well and I'm cruising, I just let it all slide, but as soon as my boss is making threatening noises or my wife pulls out her suitcase or the police start nosing around, that's when I get it together. I'm also nicer when I'm behind the eight ball. When things are going well, I get arrogant because to me that's what success is all about.

Why do we men have such a strange behavioural pattern? I think when you boil it all down, it stems from the inner conflict between being congenitally lazy but not wanting to look like an idiot. That's why competition works. It's not about winning—it's about the fear of losing and letting the world in on your lack of personal proficiency and work ethic. They say if you want to get something done, take it to someone who's busy. I say if you want to get something done, take it to someone who's in deep trouble.

CHAIN IT UP

The food chain has been in existence for millions of years, and it works well. I think we should apply the same approach to our levels of conspicuous consumption. We need a possession chain—a table that shows us the order of acquiring products and services. For example, the possession chain might tell us to start with a toaster and then move up, in time, to a toaster oven and eventually to a microwave. Starting with a microwave is in conflict with the laws of nature and will lead to unhappiness and badly burnt popcorn.

Similarly, if you live in a $250,000 home, you shouldn't be driving a $300,000 car. It will only make you unhappy. Or at least it will make the person you live with unhappy, which will eventually affect you through the trickle-down theory.

Here's a rough guide to the order in which men should spend their money: home, car, boat, motorcycle, snow machine, riding mower, Sea-Doo, bush buggy, hovercraft, backhoe, helicopter, new suit, divorce lawyer.

KIND OF INTERESTING

Over the years, the phrase "kind of" has made its way into our vernacular. The meaning of the phrase is not completely clear, and I think you have to use it with caution. Here is a list of questions for which the answer "Kind of" is inappropriate:

- Do you love me?
- Do you swear to tell the truth and nothing but the truth?
- Are you pregnant?
- Do you have a job?
- Does this car belong to you?
- Did you pay your income tax?
- Are you a doctor?
- Have you been faithful?
- Are you the father of this child?

SENSE AND SENSITIVITY

Men have been under a lot of pressure for the last thirty years or so to get more in touch with their feelings. To be more sensitive and let their feminine side come out. I guess it's a good thing. My wife's all for it, so that's pretty much the clincher around our house.

But there have been some downsides. That whole strong, silent macho man has been replaced by a bunch of gushy guys who dance just a little too well for my liking. And men who ordinarily never say anything have got in touch with their feelings, only to realize that their feelings are hurt. So they start whining. About everything. It's amazing how hundreds of years of repressed self-expression can explode into tirades on everything from the weather to squeegee kids.

Let's be careful how we use this newfound sensitivity. Some of the best male actors ever were a lot better in the silent movies than they were in the talkies.

WHAT WILL LIFE BE LIKE IN ONE HUNDRED YEARS?

- Everyone will drive disposable paper towels. They will be powered by nuclear fusion and go from zero to the speed of light in under nine seconds. Naturally, guys will try tinkering with their fusion reactors to get a little extra acceleration out of them.
- To conserve our forests, toilet paper will be replaced by the type of transporter device they had on <u>Star Trek</u>. It will instantly beam all waste into outer space. Some smart aleck will write on it, "Flush twice—it's a long way to Mars."
- Boats will use anti-gravity pods to hover a few centimetres above the water surface (so there won't be an annoying boat wake, and the hull won't be melted by toxic chemicals).
- New kinds of plastics, metal alloys, graphite compounds, ceramic materials, and paper products will mean everyone has to own 435 different blue boxes to sort their garbage.

- All jokes and all forms of comedy will be banned to prevent anyone from ever offending anyone else.
- You'll be able to eat anything you want and never get fat. This will take the fun out of eating.
- Instead of spending money, a shopper will just grab what she wants and a computer implanted in her ear will keep track of how much she owes. If someone gets too far in debt, her head will explode.
- Humans will be genetically engineered to eliminate disease, aging, and flatulence. Minor surgery such as gall bladder removal and vasectomies will be done at drive-in clinics while you sit in your car. Anyone who goes bald will have realistic-looking hair tattooed on his head. Our brains will be five times larger, creating giant headaches.
- There will be five different sexes. They still won't understand one another.
- The big debate in parenting will be whether to keep the test tube at home or have it raised in a lab.
- Everyone will switch back to Betamax.

DUMBING DOWN IN SELF-DEFENCE

The expression "dumbing down" is one I hear a lot these days. And people are worried about it. They consider dumbing down to be a form of pandering to the lowest common denominator, and the implication is that people are so stupid these days, you have to lower your intelligence level to speak to them.

I don't agree. I think the average person is smarter than ever before in history. You have to be. You have to be able to communicate with computers. The manuals are three inches thick, so there's a clue. Nobody from the Middle Ages or even the Industrial

Revolution could have handled that. They couldn't even remember their PINs. We've got voicemail, email, faxes, wireless, two-way, electronic ticketing, and on and on.

We're not dumb. We're smart. But we're tired of being smart. We need a break. We need to be dumb once in a while so our brains don't cramp. And if these big technology companies weren't run by nerds, they'd understand that. Thinking is necessary, but it's not fun. That's why smart people are boring at parties. So get with the program. Think for show but dumb down for dough.

YOUR MESSAGE IS UNIMPORTANT TO ME

Technology has allowed me to pick up some new bad habits. One of them is voicemail. If I'm too busy to answer the phone, I don't. I just let it kick over to voicemail with the idea that I'll call the person back later. Sometimes I even check the caller ID to make sure it's nobody important. Once in a while, I check the messages and then resave them because I'm too busy to call back right then. It's like the PVR. I don't have time to watch the shows I like, so I tape them, only to find out I don't have time to watch them later either.

The fundamental problem here is that technology doesn't slow down time. We don't need voicemail and email and other "advancements" that allow us to postpone commitments. We need a way to stretch time so we can do everything we want. Without that, I'm going to have to cut down on the number of television shows I like, and also on the number of friends and associates who call me and leave messages.

I'm starting to get the feeling that technology's ultimate goal is to prevent us from having friends and fun.

YOU'RE NOT FOOLING ANYONE

You may pretend to be young and in the know, but be careful. Certain actions can give you away. Here are six to watch for:

1) You buy a drink for the young lady at the end of the bar and then fall asleep before it arrives.
2) It takes you a full five minutes to get up out of the beanbag chair at your young girlfriend's apartment when the doorbell rings.
3) You wear a Monkees concert T-shirt under your Tommy Hilfiger sweater.
4) You quote one-liners from *The Tonight Show* when Jack Paar was the host.
5) When politics is being discussed, you relate everything to Watergate.
6) You have jet-black hair on your head and chin, but there's a shocking tuft of grey coming out of your left nostril.

HOW TO RUSTPROOF YOUR CAR

In the winter, the government puts so much salt on the roads that your car turns into a bag of chips. Rust chips. And come spring, when the chips are down, you'll be sitting there with a bare chassis, which is not only embarrassing but also against the law.

Now, the normal solution is to cover the rust with fibreglass, but there's a lot of work and expertise involved with that, and that puts it outside of our capabilities. So I'd like to take a fresh approach to the problem of resurfacing your automobile. I'd like you to think about linoleum. It's strong, durable, and lightweight, and if you ever get into a fender bender, a good-quality cushion floor could save your life. And it's easy to install using duct tape.

Linoleum is also very cheap, especially if you can use samples and roll ends like I do. It'll take you only a few hours on a Saturday afternoon—or any day, really—to install. But I think you'll be surprised and even amazed at the way this looks when it's all done.

And the finish comes up real nice when you use a floor polisher on there. That's more of a pride thing, though, because most linoleums have the no-wax finish, so you can just mop up any odd spill you get on it, especially if it's stuff from the kitchen, like eggs thrown at you by teenagers out of pure jealousy. That's what that is.

But what you'll have is a one-of-a-kind automobile that looks good enough to dance on. I'm sure some of you young professionals out there will be wanting to try hardwood or ceramic tiles, and if so, go right ahead. The technique is basically the same.

UNLICENSED TO THRILL

We'll all eventually come to the day when we get so old we flunk our driver's test and are no longer allowed to drive a car. This can be a major blow to the ego, so I say start preparing to beat the system now. Buy a house in a golf community on waterfront property. Then get yourself a powerboat and a golf cart—things that don't require licences. And on your ninetieth birthday, drop a racing engine into the golf cart. Then cruise the neighbourhood trying to pick up women. Preferably golfers.

TAKE A PAUSE FOR THE CAUSE

As I get older, I find that I'm not as quick to respond as I used to be. And I don't just mean in the bedroom. I mean conversationally. I remember the days when somebody would ask a question or make a controversial statement and I'd jump in there with both feet to express my opinion. I don't do that anymore. My enthusiasm for saying what I think has been dampened by experience.

A married man or anyone in middle management will tell you that there is great value in silence. The person who's talking to you will assume you're thinking very carefully about your response. She'll find that flattering. She doesn't need to know that you're actually trying to conceal your response and are taking extra time hoping she'll forget the question. If you ever have to testify in court, your lawyer will tell you to take your time and think over your answer carefully before you speak. That's good advice for daily living because you are on trial constantly.

And as soon as you testify, you have to be prepared for cross-examination.

SO MANY CARS, SO FEW LANES

It's always good when you can take something unpleasant and find value in it. Like being at a family reunion and finding that cousin who owes you money. So I was thinking that if you commute to the Big Smoke every day and are stuck in traffic for hours at a time, that's an excellent opportunity to shop for a car. You see which ones have the best acceleration. And brakes. And then acceleration again. You see which ones handle the best when switching lanes quickly or going into a four-wheel drift on the gravel shoulder. If you see a car pulled over in a radar trap, that means it has a good engine but poor visibility.

You also get a chance to do a market survey. For example, if you see a preponderance of Hondas, that means they're popular and probably have good resale value, and you'll always be able to find parts, even at the side of the road.

So instead of cursing rush hour, use it to do research for your next automotive purchase. (This technique works best when done from the window of a commuter train.)

WHEN IT'S TIME TO MOVE ON

There are times in life when it's better to keep moving. In fact, you might want to pick up the pace in situations like the following:

- There's a hint of methane in the air and it's your turn to hold the baby.
- 60 Minutes is waiting to see you in your office.
- As you arrive at your neighbour's house party, you see a large display of cleaning products.
- Young people in suits with books under their arms are standing on your front porch.
- A heavy-set man on the beach is taking off his robe.
- You see a hitchhiker dressed as Captain Kirk.
- You see a hitchhiker dressed as William Shatner.
- You see William Shatner.

I GOT REAL

I am by nature an optimist (or at least I hope I am), but there is something very empowering about removing unrealistic expectations from your life. Maybe I could bite off more than I could chew when I was young because I could hold it in my cheek for twenty years to soften it up. I don't have that kind of time anymore, so now I try to make my projections with a stronger bulb. I've stopped expecting people to do what I want. Bad weather doesn't surprise me. And I no longer make major purchases based solely on my ability to come up with the down payment.

A DOZEN EXCUSES TO GIVE THE COPS

Cops pulled you over? Cut out this list of excuses and tape it to your visor to help you talk your way out of a ticket.

1) I was speeding so I could get home before you set up this radar trap.
2) I was speeding to get out of the way so you could aim your radar at the guy behind me, who was really going fast.
3) Yes, I was speeding toward you. You looked like you needed help.
4) I was speeding to beat the sunset. Both of my headlights are burnt out.
5) But, Officer, how can I signal my turns if my indicators haven't worked since I ran into that police car five months ago? I mean, let's be fair.
6) I'm the regional quality control officer for the Acme Radar Gun Company, and I'm here doing a spot check of

our product. It seems to be functioning perfectly, so my work here is done. Goodbye.

7) I tried to stop in time, but the guy ahead of me was leading too close.

8) The guy beside me was driving in my blind spot, and his horn was in my deaf spot.

9) The other driver failed to acknowledge my lack of control.

10) The other driver failed to acknowledge the possibility that I might run the stop sign.

11) The pedestrian was taking up the whole sidewalk and left me no room.

12) The other vehicle was a hazard because it was driving at the speed limit.

A DOZEN EXCUSES TO GIVE THE JUDGE

So the police didn't believe your excuses? Well, cut out this list and put it in the pocket of your best outfit, because that's what you'll wear for your court appearance.

1) Your Honour, I would have come to a complete stop, but I wanted to get out of the way of the police car that was following me.

2) I didn't need to use my signals. I turn at that corner every day.

3) Tailgating? I was trying to give him a push, but he was going too fast. Boy, you try to be helpful!

4) I speed because it wastes gas and sends a message to certain Middle Eastern powers that this great country won't be held hostage to oil interests and threats of embargo. It's basically a political act and I'm a political prisoner.

5) My radio is stuck at full volume on an all-polka station. I had to drive fast. My non-violent side was running out of time.

6) I wasn't speeding. The radar just bounced off the metal plate in my head as I bobbed to the beat of my Bobby Vinton eight-track.

7) Did you know, Judge, that the earth orbits the sun at more than 65,000 miles per hour? Compared to that, I wasn't speeding at all.

8) I saw the sign 401, but I thought it was the speed limit, not the highway number.

9) Society is to blame for giving me a driver's licence. I'm merely a victim of incompetent examiners.

10) I wasn't wearing a seat belt because I knew the cops would make me get out of the car. They always do.

11) Yes, I was swerving down the highway, but it's not easy to kill a mosquito with a coffee cup at eighty miles an hour.

12) I would never have been driving that recklessly if the police hadn't been chasing me.

THE DOWNSIDE OF COMPETENCE

Often in life, what we're told flies in the face of what we know to be true. Take, for example, the areas of professionalism and competency. We are told that everyone wants you to excel in these areas, and that whatever you do in life, it is your duty to do it to the best of your ability. But I don't think that's entirely true. Oh sure, when you need something like open-heart surgery, you want the surgeon to be competent and professional. But when it's an activity that doesn't affect you in any way—like watching your neighbour have a pool installed—you enjoy it more if the bobcat operator is incompetent and amateurish. That's because competence is boring, and incompetence is always interesting. And when it doesn't have a negative impact on your life, it's downright entertaining. So if you're hiring someone to fill a useless redundant position in your company, go with the bumbling incompetent. He'll give everybody a lot of laughs and never quit to go to a better job.

TRAFFICKING

I was driving in the middle of a pack of cars on the highway this week. We were all speeding. No problem. Suddenly, a police car pulled onto the highway and we all hit the brakes, trying to subtly ease our way down to the speed limit. Luckily, the cop didn't notice. He just thought his car must have tremendous power to be able to catch up to all of us that quickly. So we all moved at the same speed in a huge mass joined together by guilt. Thankfully, the cop got off a couple of exits later and we could all get back to breaking the law. But we're not criminals. We just think there are a couple of laws that you obey only when a policeman is present. So when officers are around we pretend we always drive at a safe speed. And they pretend to believe us. It's kind of an unspoken agreement between the two sides—like not swearing in front of your kids and vice versa.

HOW TO TELL WHEN YOU SHOULD STOP TALKING

Whenever you're talking to someone, it's important to watch his body language to make sure he considers the conversation a worthwhile investment of his time. Here are a few signs that may indicate it's time for you to stop talking:

- The listener makes that "yak yak yak" hand gesture while you're talking.
- He turns his back to you and stares at the wall.
- He blinks and his eyes stay shut.
- He grabs his nose and looks at you accusingly.
- He pretends to see someone he knows in the distance, even though you're shipwrecked on a desert island.
- He excuses himself to take a call on his cellphone, which is actually an ashtray.
- He swallows a pickled egg whole so he can be rushed to the hospital.
- He reaches to his side, hoping to find a holstered gun.

TIME CHANGES EVERYTHING

Einstein proved that time is relative, even though you may not have time for some of them. It's a theory that becomes more relevant as we age. I'd try anything in my twenties, because I knew I had lots of time to heal or apologize or do community service. But now I'm very fussy about what I spend my time doing. I'm running out of it, so it's becoming much more valuable. I used to view life as a timeless adventure. "What do you want to do?" "I don't know. What do *you* want to do?" Now I treat it as a conjugal visit. "Let's get this over with—I need my sleep."

TAKING THE BS OUT OF CEOs

As I was washing a thin layer of ash and metal particulate off my boat last week, I got thinking about pollution and how people will say anything for money. Yes, the CEO of that big factory insists that all its emissions are inert and harmless. But he says that from his hermetically sealed office just prior to jumping into his Mercedes and speeding home to his million-dollar house—which is forty miles away and upwind. Well, I've come up with a plan to make sure these people are telling us the truth.

The Queen has to live in Buckingham Palace, the president has to live in the White House, and ministers have to live in the manse. It comes with the job. I say that CEOs of polluting companies should have to live on the grounds of their own factories. That would cut through the rhetoric pretty fast. Being ordered to live in the environment they create is a great way to force people to be honest. (With the apparent exception of those in the White House.)

HOW TO MEASURE WIND VELOCITY

It's important to know how windy it is if you plan to fish, sail, hang-glide, or wear a toupee. Meteorologists (who know nothing about Meteors, even though they were darned decent cars) measure wind speed using the Beaufort wind scale, invented by Admiral Francis Beaufort in the 1800s (which is called the nineteenth century—go figure).

Beaufort based his scale on the amount of canvas that a full-rigged frigate could carry. I don't have a frigate—although I have been known to say something similar. So I use the Wind-o-meter Scale.

Code #	Wind Speed (Knots)	Description
0	0–1	Calm. Too calm. People get edgy. Smoke from the BBQ rises straight up, attracting buzzards. You can smell yourself.
1	2–3	Light air. Leaves on trees don't move. Smoke from BBQ rises at a slight angle. You can still smell yourself.
2	4–7	Light breeze. Leaves on trees move. You can smell the guy next to you.
3	8–12	Gentle breeze. Everyone can smell everyone. Oriental wind chimes get on your nerves.
4	13–18	Moderate breeze. Nuns make flapping sound. Leaves fly all over your yard.
5	19–24	Fresh breeze. Leaves fly all over your neighbour's yard. He yells at you, but you claim you can't hear him over the wind chimes.
6	25–31	Strong breeze. Difficult to walk. Drunks are blown over. Smoke from BBQ blows horizontally, right into your eyes.
7	32–38	Moderate gale. Trees move moderately. Boring uncle asks, "Windy enough for you?" Cheeks flap when you yawn. Aluminum patio furniture on the move.

8 - - - - - 39–46 - - - - - - - - Fresh gale. Nuns blow over. Falling-down drunks are held upright. Clothes blow off clothesline. BBQ is blown over—smoke from burning deck blows horizontally. Trees move rapidly.

9 - - - - - 47–54 - - - - - - - - Strong gale. Trees move slowly—across your lawn. Boring uncle says, "Windy? This is nothing. When I was young . . ." Your favourite toque blows off.

10 - - - - 55–63 - - - - - - - - Whole gale. Your favourite shirt blows off. Neighbour's gas BBQ comes through your window. Your newly sodded lawn is now someone else's newly sodded lawn.

11 - - - - 64–75 - - - - - - - - Storm. You regret not hiring a pro to build your chimney. Boring uncle claims, "I've seen worse!" and is carried off by wind. People in trailer parks appear on nightly news. Your underwear blows off.

12 - - - - Over 75 - - - - - - - Hurricane. Your underwear blows off while you're indoors. People from trailer parks fly past your house. Your nose hairs whistle even when you're not breathing. You can't close your eyes. Even if you wanted to.

MAKING AN OLD FRIEND

I recently made a new friend who's six years older than me. He's bright and fit and has all his hair. He may even have some of mine. He's witty and laughs easily and the women seem to warm to him. Other guys in my situation might be jealous, but not me. This guy gives me hope. I think to myself that when I get to his age, I'll be just like that. I get thinking that the current balding, overweight, boring me is just a phase I'm going through, and if I can just wait it out by finding an interesting hobby like watching television, I'll eventually change from a slug in a grungy cocoon to a stylish butterfly like my new buddy. Maybe old age is like going through puberty. But in reverse.

THE GAB OF GIFTS

Always take a close look at any gift you receive on your birthday or at Christmastime because it might well contain a hidden message. Here are a few examples:

- A full-length mirror
- A comb
- Dry-cleaning coupons
- A car air freshener
- A tube of whitening toothpaste
- A dog-training DVD
- A job offer in Africa
- A skateboard
- Nose hair clippers
- A gift pack of bath soap and disinfectant
- A lawn mower

KEEP IT IN THE FAMILY

In my experience, nothing is all good or all bad. It's always a mix of the two in various quantities. Even good manners can have a bad side. I'm thinking about the good manners of not arguing with a family member who is always spouting his theories of human behaviour and galactic interaction. I know it may be impolite to disagree, but by saying nothing, we are implying to Uncle Bob that we agree with him, and that can be a very dangerous message. His ridiculous viewpoints get even more entrenched and his determination to express them increases. When you see a loudmouth in person or on television, you can be pretty sure he comes from a family of people who were just too darned polite for their own good. So if you've got someone like that in your house, please be rude to him at every opportunity. Otherwise, you're forcing the rest of us to do it for you, and that's not polite.

SMOKE FROM YOUR CAR AND WHAT IT MEANS

Smoke from the Grill, Rad, or Hoses

This is actually not smoke. It's steam. It can be caused by one of two things: Something Being There or Something Not Being There.

The Something Being There category includes anything that overheats the engine or impedes the flow of water through the engine cooling system, such as a small dead rodent or work sock wedged inside one of the hoses; a seventy-five-foot house trailer hooked to the rear bumper of a Nash Metropolitan on the upside of Pikes Peak; a gaping hole in the rad as the result of rear-ending a pole vaulter; a solid block of ice clogging the rad tubing (mainly in winter); the desert sun at noon in July; a large, furry rodent-type creature embedded in the radiator cooling fins; a thermostat rusted shut from never being serviced or replaced in the thirty years the car has been in your family.

The Something Not Being There category obviously includes the disappearance of anything necessary to allow the flow of water, such as a complete lack of said water; the absence of anti-freeze in the water (see "solid block of ice" above); the missing drive belt for the water pump; the hoses you took off to make a tuba for your sister's wedding.

Smoke from the Dashboard

Unless you're driving an early experimental car that runs on wood, dashboard smoke is probably an electrical fire. In most cases, it's caused by driver negligence: a spilled cup of coffee or even more volatile liquid, or coins dropped down the defroster vents. Maybe you dropped tinsel down there on your way home from Liberace's estate sale. Or maybe you've been impatient with the radio or heater performance and have randomly kicked under the dashboard with steel-toed shoes. Perhaps you've driven through piles of leaves for fun, shredding dried pine cones on the red-hot heater core.

In any case, you have a short-circuit causing a wire to overheat and burn. It will probably blow a fuse and go out. Or it could go out once the wire burns and opens the circuit. Or it could turn into a massive automotive fire that totally engulfs your car. But you've got a two-out-of-three chance that it's not serious, so just roll down the window and keep driving.

Smoke from the Engine Crankcase

When you see smoke coming out of the dipstick hole or the oil filler cap, that means you have a fire in the engine crankcase. If you're wondering what that is, think back to the oil fires in Kuwait. That's basically what's going on in there, except that no one will help you put it out. The engine has overheated and ignited the oil, which is usually caused by an extreme shortage of oil, which is usually caused by you buying self-serve gas and not checking the oil for seven years. If you have a crankcase fire, pull over, remove the licence plates and all other identifying features, and find an alternative mode of transportation (see tips on hitchhiking).

Smoke from the Trunk

Unless you're hauling manure, this is probably a fire. Before you open the trunk lid, try to remember what's in there. A lawn mower? Fireworks? Any type of missile? Maybe you're better off just to keep driving and keep the fire behind you. It could be burning for a while because the gas tank is back there, but on the bright side, nobody will tailgate you.

Smoke from the Wheels

Smoke from the wheels is very rarely a fire. It is usually rubber burning from friction, which 90 percent of the time is caused by you pushing down too hard on one of the pedals—either the gas or the brake. Ease back on your stops and starts, and that should remove the tire-smoking problem. It could also be that one of your rear wheels has locked up. That usually happens when an ordinary guy tries to change his own differential fluid. Remove the cover and look inside, and you'll recover that wrench you've been missing. Take it out and everything should be fine.

If it's the front tires that are smoking, you may have an alignment problem. Turn the steering wheel to go straight and get out and look at the tires. If they are pointing directly toward or away from each other, you need a front-end alignment. And so does your car.

Smoke from the Exhaust Pipe

If it's a cold or a damp day, this is probably steam and nothing to worry about. However, if the smoke is black and full of charred metal slivers with the occasional multicoloured flame ball, there could be a problem. The exhaust pipe is the off-ramp for the unburned gases from the engine. Be careful what kind of gas you use. Don't buy it on the black market from a guy with a German accent. His prices are way out of line. And don't just assume that old cans of paint and hairspray and homemade beer will automatically work in your car. Take your exhaust problems very seriously. As all mechanics and proctologists know, there is no better clue to how things are working than what comes out the back end.

Smoke from the Back Seat

When you notice smoke coming from the back seat, you have to remember if you have thrown anything over your shoulder in the past few hours. A lit cigarette? A cigarette lighter? A propane torch? Bowls of kerosene? The Olympic flame? A BBQ? Church candles? Roman candles? Cans of napalm?

If the answer is no, then check to see if anybody's back there. If you discover a passionate couple, find out their ages. If they're between forty and seventy, look out—it's smoke. If they're under forty, relax—it's steam. If they're over seventy, ignore it—it's dust.

THE UNKINDEST CUT

I know many factors make people what they are, but chemistry has to be a big part of it. And if you're a man, testosterone must be the most influential chemical. If you take a normal man and drastically reduce his testosterone level, you get either an ugly woman or a guy who walks funny and never shaves. Testosterone is a key ingredient in the man recipe, and that's why I'm concerned about the negative messages that we see targeting testosterone every day. Take, for example, all those ads to promote animals being neutered.

Now, I can understand the rationale of castrating pigs to fatten them up in the belief that they'll eat more if they have nothing else to think about, but the idea of having your dog neutered to make him more manageable upsets me. Some days I'm a little unmanageable myself, and I don't want my wife looking at our friendly, obedient dog and getting ideas.

NO NEED TO EXPLAIN, EVEN IF YOU COULD

There are many great things about being married to the same person for a long time, and I'm a grateful husband on a fairly regular basis. One of the best perks is the evolution of communication between two people over time. It eventually reaches the point where words are unnecessary. What a bonus! Life is hard enough, but having to explain every little setback or accident—or why the police are in the driveway—can get very tedious. I truly appreciate being able just to go quietly to bed with a couple of aspirins and a cold compress. It's great to be with someone who knows you so well that you don't need to come up with an explanation. The downside of that relationship is that when you've screwed up so badly that you do have to come up with an explanation, it had better be a dandy.

THE MEN'S ROOMS

While men and women are doing more things together than ever, which is a good thing, there is obviously still a need for each to spend time with their own kind—to be with people who share their physiology and experiences and, in many cases, attitudes. Women seem to do this much better than men do. They have shopping trips or quilting bees or spa days or sleepovers. The list for men is less impressive: hunting and fishing. We seem to have to be killing something to have a good time. And men having a sleepover really gets the rumour mill going. So instead, why don't we start a men's club where we could relax and be ourselves and bond? Here are some suggested features:

- The TV Room: Built on top of an open dumpster. The television screen occupies one whole wall, and everybody gets a remote.
- The BS Lounge: You're allowed to tell any story you want, and nobody has to pretend to believe it.
- The Observation Room: Men sit in elevated bleachers and watch other members assemble items without reading the instructions.
- The Garage: A place where men lean under the open hood of a car, beer in hand, staring blankly at the fuel injection system.
- The Model Room: A pool for racing model boats and a slot car track. Reckless speed with limited liability.
- The Decompression Room: No eye contact. No talking. No chairs facing each other.
- The Hot Stove Lounge: A place to burn things, including trees, old furniture, unsuccessful projects.
- The Underwear Room: Relaxed dress code.

TO SEE OURSELVES AS OTHERS SEE US

I was at a social event and a fat, bald middle-aged guy was pointing out all the beautiful single young women who were at the event. And he capped it off with "Just my luck, I'm married." And he was so right.

YOU ARE A USED CAR

If you live with someone who's an avid shopper, you may need to be extra careful with your appearance and behaviour. A person who shops a lot knows the importance of comparing features and options, and is completely focused on getting good value. And the scariest part is that she continues to comparison shop even after she's bought the item. If she sees something she likes better or the product doesn't perform as advertised, she has no qualms about taking it back for a refund. This can be a dangerous pattern if you happen to be the husband of such a person.

My advice is for you to see yourself as a used car. You can go one of two ways: you can either try to convince your wife that you have retained so much of your original value that she'd never find a better unit of your vintage, or you can convince her that you have zero trade-in value and the only way she'll get her money out of you is to run you into the ground.

CIVILIZATION BEGINS AT HOME

I heard on the radio this week that scientists are looking for house designs that would work well on Mars. The implication is that we're going to live on Mars soon because earth is getting overpopulated. I beg to differ. New York and Toronto may be overpopulated, but have you been to Alaska lately? We have lots of room left right here on earth. It's just that most of our available space doesn't have perfect weather or soil and isn't close to a major highway or an indoor mall. But then, neither is Mars and it's a heck of a commute. Maybe one day some of us will live there, but I'd take a hard look at Baffin Island first.

HOW TO MAKE THE MOST OF YOURSELF

You can't do a lot about your basic physical appearance, but you can enhance how you look by the way you dress and the environment in which you place yourself. Here are a few suggestions:

- If you're short, fill your garden with dwarf plants and stand by the ceramic leprechaun.
- If you're on the heavy side, hang out near short, wide buildings.
- If you're extra tall, look up all the time.
- If your eyes are crossed, paint something interesting on the end of your nose.
- If you're very thin, lean on telephone poles.
- If your teeth are yellow, dye your beard brown.
- If you have halitosis, exhale slowly upwind.
- The uglier you are, the more cologne you should wear.
- The more wrinkled you are, the more ironed your clothes have to be.

HOW TO MAKE A DUAL-PURPOSE PATIO SET

It's hard to save money if you don't have any, so the next best thing is to save money by finding new ways to use things you already own. For example, if you have a home with a door and a couple of window awnings and a television antenna, you can make an attractive, cost-effective patio set. In the winter, the house will look the way it does now; in the summer, it will look quite different. Let's say you're starting with a house that looks like this:

Diagram A
From now on, this is how your house will look in the winter only.

Step One

Remove the television antenna. Nobody watches TV in the summer anyway. Now, you could climb up on the roof to remove it, but it's very time-consuming to get the ladder back from the neighbour and climb all the way up there and then have to lie for an hour in the shrubs waiting for the ambulance. So I recommend you throw your boat anchor up on the roof and try to hook it around the antenna pole. If you have a lot of anchor rope, you might want to clear the other side of the house of kids and lawn ornaments.

Once you have the anchor hooked to the antenna, attach the other end of the rope to whichever one of your car bumpers has the least amount of rust. After you tie it on, bring the vehicle as close as possible to the house to create slack in the rope. (When removing a television antenna, you rely heavily on the element of surprise.) Nail the gas pedal. As soon as the rope snaps tight, the unit should be picked cleanly off the roof.

Step Two

You have to change the shape of the antenna for our purposes. Be careful. You don't want to alter the reception capabilities of the frequency-tuned components. Hold the antenna like a battering ram and run it into the inside corner of your garage as shown in Diagram B.

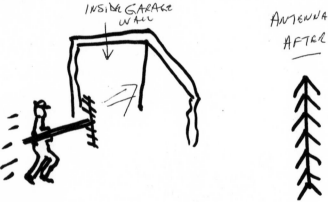

Diagram B
Ram it as many times as necessary until it looks like the picture.

Step Three

You need a front door with a doorknob right in the middle. These doors were extremely popular for about nine days in the early sixties, and you'll need to find a house built during that time to find this type of door. The easiest way is to tell a real estate agent that you're looking to buy a house with the front doorknob in the middle of the door. When he takes you through one, check the walls for a calendar that has the vacation trip to Opryland marked, so you'll know when to drop back around to get the door. Install it in your own house and then remove the doorknob, leaving a hole in the centre of the door.

Step Four

This next step is a little dangerous because you have to drive on the highway. At night. Without your headlights on. Don't come back until you have two of those triangular yield signs. Take an adjustable wrench with you. And have a really interesting story to tell the highway patrol, just in case.

Step Five

Using duct tape, attach the yield signs to the door as shown in Diagram C.

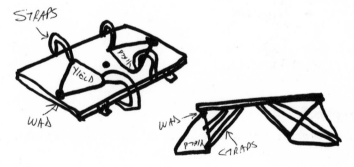

Diagram C

The wad of duct tape at the point works as a hinge. The strips of tape to the corners prevent the signs from swinging out too far. Once they're attached, flip the door over and let the signs swing into place as shown. The door is now a patio table.

Step Six

Remove the pair of awnings from the windows. You can use either a screwdriver or an adjustable wrench, or if you're pressed for time, the boat anchor technique is always quick and effective. Next, duct-tape the awnings together and slide them over the bent antenna and down into the doorknob hole as shown in Diagram D.

Diagram D

You're now ready to enjoy a full summer of outdoor entertaining. When winter comes, simply reverse the steps and move indoors.

Diagram E
Beautiful patio set in summer

Diagram F
Normal house in winter

TO DYE FOR

I know a lot of guys my age are dyeing their hair. That's fine. I think it's important for people to look their best. But there is a risk involved. Anything you do to make yourself look younger, if successful, will attract younger people to you. Younger friends and co-workers and even potential love interests will gravitate toward you, and that could create problems. The friends and co-workers will want to do things that are completely outside your experience. You'll be in trouble. You can't fake skydiving. And it's even worse with a love interest. You can't fake anything. And the last thing you need is a young girlfriend who will cut into your hair-dyeing time. With luck, she'll actually turn out to be a woman your own age who also dyes her hair. That will give you both a common interest and something you can do together on the weekends.

FORGIVE WHAT?

I've always had difficulty with the phrase "Forgive and forget." I think it's a great idea, but it's one of those phrases—"I promise I'll respect you in the morning" is another—that seldom happens. I'm just not spiritually evolved enough to forgive and forget. I was feeling bad about that until I realized that it's not really necessary to forgive *and* forget. All you have to do is forget. If you can forget that somebody did something, that's good enough. You don't have to forgive them, because you have no idea what you'd even be forgiving them for. This has given me new hope. Forgiving has always been difficult, but forgetting is something I just seem to get better and better at.

CARS OF THE FUTURE

I'm looking to buy a new car in the near future, and it's turning into a real life moment for me. I've started to realize that since they're making cars that last ten years, I won't need a whole lot more of them. That changes everything. That means I'd better make sure I get a car I feel good about. I don't want to end my days in a Yugo. No, I'm thinking I'd better get that sports car I've always wanted. The clock is ticking here. So I went looking at Corvettes.

I noticed the salesman trying to look away as I struggled for a full five minutes to get into the vehicle. But that was like a blink of an eye compared to the time it took me to get out. And while I was in there—lying about three inches off the ground in the prone position—I didn't look like a macho racer at the Indy 500. I looked like an old guy on a stretcher. People would think I was driving my grandson's car.

And on the self-preservation level, bad things happen when

reflexes like mine are going more than a hundred miles an hour. I'm calling the salesman today and ordering a small, gutless sedan with plastic doors and airbags. Please don't say, "You are what you drive."

DRESS SENSE

I'm having a problem with my closet these days: it's full of clothes that I never wear. I spent an hour or so looking at the situation, trying to figure out what went wrong, and it seems to be a combination of factors.

First of all, there are the clothes that my wife has bought for me. These tend to be at the stylish, suave, Euro-dork end of the spectrum, and they're always bought when she's been to a movie or read a romance novel and has forgotten what I look like.

Then there are the clothes that I bought while shopping with my wife. These purchases are always made in a hurry, without trying anything on, and for the sole purpose of satisfying her and getting out of the store as quickly as possible. They may look nice, but they rarely come anywhere near to fitting me.

Then we have the small group of clothes that actually fit me. I refuse to wear these because they're made for a much fatter, older man.

That leaves us with the clothes that I actually do wear, and they're all at least ten years old. They tend to be a little tight, and sometimes I have to suck in my stomach so hard that I get back spasms. But I hate to throw them out because guys like me prefer a wardrobe that's been lived in. So instead, I came up with a plan. All I need to do is meet a guy my age who's my height and age but ten pounds heavier. Then I'll throw out everything I have now and buy all his old clothes.

HOW TO RECYCLE AN ENGINE AS KITCHENWARE

If you're like me, you hate to throw anything out—boxes, string, or automobile engines. I have an engine out back that I could take down to the scrap metal dealer and get a few dollars for, but it wouldn't be worth my time to load it into the back of the truck and drive all the way down there. So what do we do with an old engine? Well, before you drive to a provincial park and dump it down a ravine, let me show you how one motor can outfit your whole kitchen.

Everybody who has space between their teeth likes corn on the cob. And parts from a car engine can give you an interesting way to serve it. Use a couple of valves as cob holders and fill up the valve cover with melted butter. Or 10W-30 if it's to go.

The air filter makes a handy saucepan for frying. And of course the lid comes with it. If you tighten the wing nut on there, it makes it into a pressure cooker. Just imagine it bursting at the seams with the smell of pressurized yams.

And I don't care how far you go, you're not going to find a better roasting pan with a built-in drain plug than the crankcase cover off the bottom of the engine. You roast a turkey in that and you'll taste the difference, believe me. It's greasy eatin', but it's good eatin'.

If you're serving soup to a large number of guests, the exhaust manifold cuts ladling to a quarter of the regular time. Just line up the exhaust ports on the manifold with your four soup bowls and pour the soup down your own tailpipe.

And you were going to throw all this out! Where else are you going to find a free set of kitchenware that has over a hundred thousand miles on it? That's unique, isn't it? And Mother's Day is just around the corner.

WHAT MAKES MEN DIFFERENT FROM WOMEN? THAT'S THE $3,100 QUESTION

Not all the differences between the sexes are simply to do with fashion, haircuts, and male oppression. Even the most ardent feminists will agree that men are physically different from women. And as the French say, "*Vive la différence.*" Which translates to "I'll show you mine if you'll show me yours." (See now, some women wouldn't find that funny. That's got to be biological.)

According to scientists (real scientists, not those actors wearing lab coats in the laxative commercials), women and men have physically different brains. More of a woman's brain is devoted to processing words, while a man has more of the grey matter working on shapes and geometry. That's why men have trouble describing what they want and would rather just build it and then throw it out if it's not right. That's also why they have trouble explaining what went wrong, whereas their wives seem to be able to name all kinds of stupid mistakes.

You can see the many areas where men are superior by studying their behavioural patterns.

1) *Men have better spatial sense than women.* For example, no woman would ever attempt to build a $3,100 garage without a level or a measuring tape simply because she can "eyeball" it.

2) *Men have more sensitive eyesight than women.* For example, I can see all the things wrong with our old garage, whereas my wife doesn't seem to notice any problems.

3) *Men are better drivers than women.* Especially with stuff like bulldozers, which we could use very easily to knock down the old garage if our wives would let us.

4) *Men are better at math.* For example, I know that spending $3,100 to replace our garage, even though it has at least ten

more years of life in it, actually makes economic sense in the long run considering interest rates and amortization and depreciation and good clean fun. My wife disagrees.

5) *Men are better at judging units of time.* For example, I can mentally calculate that even though the weekend is almost over, I could have our old garage torn down and the new one well under construction by sunset, and I'd finish it next weekend.

6) *Men are better at performing multiple tasks.* For example, even if I don't get the garage done next weekend, I'll do it along with the half-finished boat, the half-finished trellis, the fence I started, the leaky bedroom ceiling I haven't finished patching, the toilet I haven't totally replaced, and the nine other jobs I have on the go.

7) *Men have better spatial-projection abilities.* I swear I can just picture how great a new garage will look, whereas my wife can't see what a difference it would make.

8) *Men think more logically.* For example, my wife thinks it's crazy to spend $3,100 and tear down a perfectly good garage, but I can see all the benefits. Still, no matter how many times I explain them, she feels that having a brighter, cleaner place to store those old oil drums is not a major priority.

These are just the most obvious areas of male dominance that deserve scientific research or a study. I would be willing to undertake the study if someone gives me, say, $3,100.

CREDIT WHERE CREDIT IS DUE

They have sophisticated computers in cars these days. Things like the GPS that tells you exactly how to get to where you're going, for anyone who doesn't have a wife. Or the central monitoring unit that tells you if there's a door open or a seat belt undone or your engine just fell out. So I'm thinking they could easily devise a computer to keep track of how fast you're going compared to the speed limit. For example, if you're driving to work and the speed limit is sixty, but you're only going thirty because the traffic is so bad, that would be registered in the computer. Let's say you did that for fifteen minutes. The computer would show that as a credit on the dashboard screen, and as soon as you hit an open stretch of road, you'd be allowed to use that credit without getting a speeding ticket. You could go 90 for fifteen minutes or 120 for seven and a half minutes or 150 for three and three-quarters minutes or the speed of light for a nanosecond. As soon as your credit was used up, you would resume the speed limit.

I know this would never work, but it's nice to dream about.

WHAT'S IN IT FOR HER?

You ever see these old guys with the young ex-model wives? He's a shrivelled-up billionaire and she's gorgeous and the same age as his socks. They call them trophy wives—a little something to have on your arm to let other guys know that you have more to offer at ninety than they do at twenty-seven. (You may have more to offer, but not for nearly as long.)

Okay, I can understand the trophy concept from the old guy's point of view; I just don't see the appeal for the woman. Now, if it's love, that's fine. Logic and love rarely intersect. But if it's something else, then it seems to me that this old codger is a trophy husband for her. Some trophy! I've got bowling awards that look better than most of these guys.

I'm thinking that these women are more attracted to the safety and security of a rich grandfatherly type than they are to the good looks and virility of a man their own age. And I guess when the trophy husband passes on in a year or two, she just finds another one like him. There are a lot of rich old guys who find young women attractive. But it takes someone special to be a career trophy wife. You need the personality of a nurse and a bunch of black dresses.

NEW LEASE ON LIFE

I've just leased a car, and I found the leasing options to be interesting. The payments are about the same as they are for a car loan, but at the end of the term, I have more choices with the lease. With a loan, you may end up owning a car that you don't like. With a lease, that doesn't happen. So naturally, I was wondering if you could expand the lease theory to personal relationships. What if instead of marrying a person, you just sign a three-year lease? At the end of the term, you could re-sign for another three years, unload the person privately, or just walk away—as long as you hadn't had any accidents.

PANDORA'S TOOL BOX

Once in a while, you have to call a repairman to come and fix something in your home. In most cases, you don't know the guy and probably just picked his number out of the phone book. The problem, of course, is that you may be dealing with an incompetent who will create more problems than he corrects. Now, you don't want to be rude and ask him outright if he has any idea what he's doing, so here's a way to make a very quick judgment on the quality of the impending work: hang around and look at the contents of his tool box. If it contains any of the following, you may have a problem:

- Lots of bandages and painkillers
- A handgun
- F. Lee Bailey's business card
- Only three tools, all hammers
- A one-way plane ticket to Panama

WHAT'S YOURS IS YOURS

After you've been married for a while, your personal belongings tend to get intermingled. Sometimes, to save money or because you ran out of something, you end up using toiletries that your wife bought for herself. This can be inappropriate and sometimes harmful. For example, a razor blade that has shaved a pair of human legs is no longer safe to use on a human face. Toothpaste containing baking soda is not for the discerning palate. And you shouldn't be using Shampoo for Fine Hair when what you really need is Shampoo for Scarce Hair.

HOW TO MAKE YOUR OWN IN-CAR ENTERTAINMENT

Nothing spoils a vacation faster than kids constantly whining, "Are we there yet?" "I'm hungry. I'm bored. I think we're lost. This road stinks." Or how about all five of your youngsters chanting, "We want to stop for ice cream!" in the middle of your airline flight to Disneyland?

To make the family trip less of a screaming-and-pouting festival, there are some games to amuse the kids while you drive. Or if your kids are old enough to drive, here are some games to calm your nerves.

Word Scramble, or Dowr Marblecs

Get your kids to try to unscramble the following everyday words. For example, the first one, "Upshut," is really "Shut up." Get it? Enjoy.

UPSHUT	SINLEEC	UVIRRR
BOWKRPP	TEOFMTN	QQIFNNZE
TRVU	ZOZ	LELALILOLU
CORLWOKWZEE	PRENT	FNURB

Wasn't that fun? Now try unscrambling these common phrases used in everyday conversation:

SPLEW RRS MUBS PLUNT GNURINGLY.
YABBA DABBA DOO!
US DEFT GRILL UBU SNO TIDDUS POOTY.
SHE SMELL SEA SCHELL BY DEE SEECHORE.
KLATUX BARADE NICTO.
YUU STIPUD DOGDANT *8%!#$+#^?@!

IMA TON A NGURIELDMMGINNEGS CQOUISTNT' TURB-PELT GNU.
QUNADO OMNI FLUNKUS MORITATI.
AH! AH! AH! AH! AH! . . . WELBOT.
DOMO ARIGATO, MR. ROBOTO.
IXNAY, IT'SAY EETHAY OPSCAY!

CAR SONGS

One way to pass the time on a long family trip is to have a singalong. But most songs last only three minutes and end up with everyone arguing over what the lyrics are. I've actually seen people come to blows over the words to "Blinded by the Light" by Manfred Mann. And you don't want to be in a van full of guys singing "I Am Woman."

The ideal song for a long trip is "99 Bottles of Beer." It lasts for miles and miles. Everyone can remember the words. And everyone knows exactly how long till the end of the song. On the other hand, "Row, Row, Row Your Boat" gets monotonous pretty quickly and leads to arguments over when someone was supposed to join in with his verse. That old classic "Hello Operator, Give Me Number 9" might offend some passengers. And the popular "Hey, Bus Driver, Speed Up a Little Bit" is lots of fun until you hit a guardrail.

Since we live in such a large country with long, lonely stretches of highway with nothing to see except scenery and nature, it's obvious we need more songs for long trips. So here are a few I've written. Enjoy.

Flugelhorn

(To the tune of "Who's Afraid of the Big Bad Wolf?")

Over there in Switzerland,
Switzerland, Switzerland,
There's a funny Swiss brass band,
Swiss brass band, Swiss brass band.

They've played this way since they were born,
They were born, they were born,
By blowing on their flugelhorn,
And it sounds like this . . .

(One passenger does a trumpet solo with his lips, making a lot of wet, funny sounds while everyone else sings the chorus.)

Chorus:
Flugelhorn, flugelhorn
Bugel horn, bugel horn
Flugelhorn, flugelhorn
Bugel horn, bugel horn.

(Repeat with passengers taking turns doing the trumpet solo. The goal is to make the funniest sounds with the least spit.)

Never Heard of It

Driving along in our family car,
And we still have to go very far,
Looked out the window—guess what I saw,
Sitting there at the side of the road?

Sitting there, looking oh so fine,
On a post I saw a sign.
And so the sign I read,
And here's exactly what it said:

(At this point, someone reads what's on a passing sign.)

Never heard of that before.
Sounds really dumb, oh what a bore.
Never hope I end up there.
Whatever that is, I don't care.

(Repeat with a new sign.)

Everyone But Us

(To the tune of "London Bridge Is Falling Down")

See this car we're passing by, rolling by, rolling by?
See this car we're passing by? The people in it stink.

See the driver of that car, of that car, of that car?
What's he looking at us for? That stupid little fink.

Look at all those passengers, passengers, passengers.
All those pinheads in one car—kinda makes you think.

Let's all wave and they'll wave back, they'll wave back,
  they'll wave back.
Look, they waved right back at us! What a bunch of
  dinks.

(Repeat.)

The Gift

(Some songs involve clapping along or hand gestures and so on.
This song is sort of like that.)

I have a little gift I must pass on
To the person on my right.
Will they pass it on to the next one along?
Yes, I think they might.

My little gift is free of charge.
I made it just for you.
It's very hard and very large.
You'll feel it through and through.

It's not like any other gifts,
If I may be so bold, sir.
I make it when I take my fist
And punch you in the shoulder.

(PUNCH!)

Chorus:
Pass it on. Pass it on. To the person next to you.
Pass it on. Pass it on. Your arm is turning blue.

(Repeat from the top.)

The Door Song

(Here's another song that gets kids physically involved.)

We're heading down the highway and we're way over
    the limit.
If there's a car crash up ahead, then we will soon be in it.
But meanwhile, let's all take our minds off what fate has
    in store
By reaching down and pulling hard and opening our
    door.

Click, pull, push it open. [Everyone opens car's doors.]
See how the wind blows it shut?
Click, pull, force the door open. [Open doors.]
We look like a car full of nuts.

Flap our doors doing ninety-five— [Open doors.]
And our car looks like it's flying.
Other cars stare, but we don't care. [Open doors.]
We're laughing so hard we're crying!

How Many Facial Tissues?

How many facial tissues are there left
In this Kleenex box?
The label says there's five hundred,
But that sounds like a lot.

So far I've only pulled one out,
But wait, here is another.
I'll put it out and lay it down
Here beside its brother.

(Pull out a Kleenex and start at top of song again, changing
"one" to "two" and so on. Stop when you run out of Kleenex.)

HOW TO BUILD YOU OWN DRIVE-IN CAR

'm not talking about a car to take to the drive-in theatre, because where the theatre used to be there's now a Walmart. I'm talking about your very own self-contained drive-away, drive-in theatre, made out of your car.

Your guests will sit in the car, just like at a drive-in. But the screen will be mounted on the inside of the hood, and when the hood flips up, forward, the screen's in position.

(If you have a car where the hood opens the other way, just wail away at it with a ten pound sledge and then re-attach it properly using duct tape)

Hang your screen on the inside of the hood. You can use a bedsheet or, if you prefer something white, I suggest a fridge door.

Mount your projector on the rear deck behind the back seat. (You may have to move the dog with the blinking eyes) Attach the power cord to the car's battery.

While you're there, dump a bag of unpopped popcorn kernels into the hole in the exhaust manifold. Once you start the engine and the manifold heats up, the popcorn will pop and be blown out the exhaust. You can catch it by clipping a pair of panty hose over the end of your tailpipe.

Keep cold drinks and chocolate bars in the trunk and you have your very own portable drive-in slide theatre.

(If you are ever pulled over by the police, be sure to tell them that this was all your idea).

MARRIAGE: THE TAXPAYER'S REVENGE

I was at my accountant's recently, and he was telling me that when a husband (or wife) passes on, there's no tax to be paid as long as he leaves his entire estate to his spouse. Then when that surviving spouse passes on, all taxes become due and payable. Suddenly a light bulb went off in my head. If the surviving spouse remarries immediately and then leaves everything to the new spouse, the tax benefits continue. And if that new person is a lot younger than the surviving spouse, the benefits go on for a long, long time. Now I know why you often see an old guy with a really young second wife. That ain't no lady—that's a tax shelter.

THE SLIDING SCALE

I sometimes find it amazing that we all have such differing opinions about each other. I think it's because we pay so much attention to ourselves. We look in the mirror a lot, think about things, and try to figure out problems. We often listen much more intently to what we have to say on a subject, because we consider our comments to be the highlight of any conversation. We are very familiar with ourselves physically, mentally, and spiritually, so we become the yardstick by which we judge the world around us. When we say someone is smart or attractive, we really mean "by comparison." For example, I think Regis Philbin is a pretty smart guy, but would Albert Einstein have felt the same way about him? Of course, the corollary to this theory is that you're going to be judged the same way. You will seem smart only to people who are dumber than you, and you will seem attractive only to people who are uglier than you. You might want to keep that in mind when you're looking for friends or soulmates. Of course, occasionally you see an exception—in my case, you find an ugly guy married to a beautiful woman—but that's not science, that's love. Or martyrdom.

LAST WORD

I thought I'd end this book with one last word to all you middle-aged guys out there who, for one reason or another, have abandoned your dreams. Maybe you dreamed of being an astronaut and ended up a space cadet. Maybe you dreamed of being an award-winning statesman and ended up a ward of the state. Maybe you dreamed of being an Amway salesman and you are.

Whatever the disappointment, at this time in our lives we shouldn't be bitter. Maybe we set our goals too high. Personally, I wanted to set the world land speed record in a rocket car that I designed, engineered, and built. But in retrospect, my dream was a bit of a long shot. Especially after I dropped out of junior high.

As we head into the last half of our lives, we should still be ambitious, but we need more realistic dreams. Like vowing to go to your grave with at least one of your own teeth. Or doing something nice for someone every day, even if it's just refraining from telling them what you're thinking. I'll follow my dreams no matter how old or worn out I get. Even if I end up in a wheelchair. In fact, I'm designing one with a rocket engine.

COMING SOON!

HERE ARE SOME OF THE MANY INTERESTING AND ENTERTAINING THINGS YOU WILL FIND IN THE NEXT RED GREEN BOOK***

- The Intricacies of Hang-Gliding and How to Make a Leg Splint
- The Importance of Intimidation When Running a Service Business
- Friendly Ways of Keeping the Neighbours the Hell off Your Property
- Avoiding Activity as a Lifestyle
- The Importance of Excess Gas in the Need to Find Your Own Space
- The Exciting New Technologies That Are Coming Soon, and How to Sound Like You Understand Them
- The Importance of Pretending You Are Interested in Other People
- How to Get Your Wife and Kids to Do What You Want So You Can Have More Family Time Together
- How to Cook a Three-Course Meal and How to Scrape It off the Ceiling
- Red Reviews the Toshiba 486DX Laptop with Active Matrix Monitor and Built-in Fax/Modem
- How to Turn Your Van into a Bed and Breakfast

*** Unless the publisher continues to reject great ideas.

ALSO BY RED GREEN

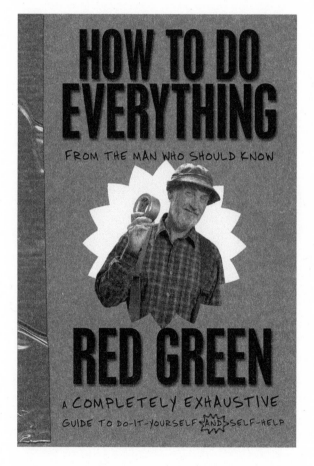

HOW TO DO EVERYTHING

FROM THE MAN WHO SHOULD KNOW

RED GREEN

A COMPLETELY EXHAUSTIVE

GUIDE TO DO-IT-YOURSELF AND SELF-HELP

Anchor Canada | 978-0-385-66775-3| $19.95